"Old people are useless"

Darren Blakeborough

"Old people are useless"

Representations of Aging on The Simpsons

Lambert Academic Publishing

Impressum/Imprint (nur für Deutschland/ only for Germany)

Bibliografische Information der Deutschen Nationalbibliothek: Die Deutsche Nationalbibliothek verzeichnet diese Publikation in der Deutschen Nationalbibliografie; detaillierte bibliografische Daten sind im Internet über http://dnb.d-nb.de abrufbar.

Alle in diesem Buch genannten Marken und Produktnamen unterliegen warenzeichen-, marken- oder patentrechtlichem Schutz bzw. sind Warenzeichen oder eingetragene Warenzeichen der jeweiligen Inhaber. Die Wiedergabe von Marken, Produktnamen, Gebrauchsnamen, Handelsnamen, Warenbezeichnungen u.s.w. in diesem Werk berechtigt auch ohne besondere Kennzeichnung nicht zu der Annahme, dass solche Namen im Sinne der Warenzeichen- und Markenschutzgesetzgebung als frei zu betrachten wären und daher von jedermann benutzt werden dürften.

Verlag: Lambert Academic Publishing AG & Co. KG
Theodor-Heuss-Ring 26, 50668 Köln, Deutschland
Telefon +49 681 3720-310, Telefax +49 681 3720-3109, Email: info@lap-publishing.com

Herstellung in Deutschland:
Schaltungsdienst Lange o.H.G., Berlin
Books on Demand GmbH, Norderstedt
Reha GmbH, Saarbrücken
Amazon Distribution GmbH, Leipzig
ISBN: 978-3-8383-1651-2

Imprint (only for USA, GB)

Bibliographic information published by the Deutsche Nationalbibliothek: The Deutsche Nationalbibliothek lists this publication in the Deutsche Nationalbibliografie; detailed bibliographic data are available in the Internet at http://dnb.d-nb.de.

Any brand names and product names mentioned in this book are subject to trademark, brand or patent protection and are trademarks or registered trademarks of their respective holders. The use of brand names, product names, common names, trade names, product descriptions etc. even without a particular marking in this works is in no way to be construed to mean that such names may be regarded as unrestricted in respect of trademark and brand protection legislation and could thus be used by anyone.

Publisher:
Lambert Academic Publishing AG & Co. KG
Theodor-Heuss-Ring 26, 50668 Köln, Germany
Phone +49 681 3720-310, Fax +49 681 3720-3109, Email: info@lap-publishing.com

Copyright © 2009 Lambert Academic Publishing AG & Co. KG and licensors
All rights reserved. Saarbrücken 2009

Printed in the U.S.A.
Printed in the U.K. by (see last page)
ISBN: 978-3-8383-1651-2

Table of Contents

List of Tables

INTRODUCTION

Homer: Hmm...sorry, Dad. You're too old.

Abe: [*stammers*] Too old? Why, that just means I have experience. Who chased the Irish out of Springfield village in aught four? Me, that's who!

Irish man: And a fine job you did, too.

Homer: Aw, Dad. You've done a lot of great things, but you're a very old man now, and old people are useless. [*tickles Abe*] Aren't they? Aren't they? Huh? Yes they are! Yes they are! Tee hee --

Abe: Stop it! That's a form of abuse.

(Swartzwelder, 1994, January 6)[1]

As words on a piece of paper, Homer Simpson's response to his aging father Abraham Simpson[2] sounds callous and derogatory. When Homer exclaims "...you're a very old man now, and old people are useless", it is a sentiment—or at least representative of a sentiment—to aging that is increasingly echoed in modern western culture. Cultural stereotypes abound which portray the elderly as senile, feeble, frail, financially distressed, lonely, non-productive members of society, or some other social problem. Existing research and numerous communications theories indicate that the mass media is largely

---

[1] All quotes and/or scripts used throughout this thesis are either transcribed by the researcher directly from video or DVD or else taken from the exhaustive Simpsons Archive: Episode Capsules at http://www.snpp.com/ unless otherwise noted.
[2] Grampa Simpson, Abraham Simpson, Abe, and Grampa will all be used interchangeably to refer to the same character.

responsible in helping to construct and transmit the ideologies that both young and old hold toward the aging process. This can pose problems in many different facets of society as some report that "factual information about aging is rarely...presented in popular media" (Weaver, 1994, p. 479). Many elderly people cite this as a primary issue with media representations of age.

The exclusion of what is seen as a realistic portrayal of aging leaves many of our elders feeling that their lives, and wealth of lived experience aren't accurately depicted in movies, TV, print, music, or advertising. Others still feel that they are not only portrayed unrealistically but actually have had their voices ignored altogether (Healey and Ross, 2002). Many are beginning to express concern that the media is presenting an alternate reality to aging and presenting an unfavourable influence over viewers. As a major socializing agent, TV helps to convey the images and ideals that ultimately help to construct our social fabric. If the media exclude, stereotypically portray, show them as less than active members of society or misrepresent the elderly in another fashion, this is the message the majority of the viewing public internalizes.

The argument that media images of aging are evolving into a more positive look at the elderly is emerging from new research. These studies seem to purport the notion that these positive images of the elderly are directly tied to consumer culture and product consumption. The elderly—at least the young-old—are viewed as an incredibly attractive emerging market with burgeoning resources and little debt (Sawchuk, 1995; Tulle-Winton, 1999). Featherstone and Hepworth (1995) identify a new ideal emerging where the idea of "the elderly" isn't a sufficient label for all purposes, particularly marketing, and as such this group has been bifurcated (and potentially more so) into "young-old and old-old". This is important when marketing to the young-old as it "rarely depicts the old-old associations between 'deep old age', terminal illness, and death" (p. 44). So it is important to take from this the idea that the new breed of positive imagery does nothing to dispel the negative discourse on aging, it simply suggests how a good or a service can seemingly help to subvert this "horrible" process. But is there an avenue for positive imagery on aging to exist outside of the consumption model? Relying primarily on theoretical writings beginning with Frederic Jameson's postmodern aesthetic and bridging it with Linda Hutcheon's work on parody and irony, this book will demonstrate how television's The Simpsons can be looked at as such an arena.

This book is assembled in such a way as to take the reader through a view of how aging studies, identity theories, media studies, postmodern theory, and The Simpsons are inter-related in these questions of representation. This text examines the broad scholarship in aging studies as it relates to the larger questions posed here. By identifying that our population is aging and the social concerns this raises, the media and its role in the transmission of ideological imagery can be examined, and is. A wealth of research is reviewed that looks at representations of elder individuals in movies, on TV, in music, and on the silver screen that identifies problems with negative portrayals and under-representation versus the larger population.

The next issue examined is how these representations relate to notions of elderly self conception and identity. Do the images that elderly individuals see in mass media influence how they see themselves? How they see others on their cohort? While many theories of identity purport to answer these and other questions, postmodern theory with its notion of a fragmented, unfixed identity shows these politics of identity are vast, constantly in flux, and unstable. It is here that the next step is made into that larger sea of postmodernity.

The theory chapter tackles the background, emergence, and growth of postmodern theoretical thought along with its tenets and implications. Moving from the larger theoretical model into questions of aesthetics, Frederic Jameson's work is central in most investigations of postmodern aesthetics, even if only to counter his widely quoted views. As one of the pre-eminent, modern day Marxist critics, Jameson's seminal work in *Postmodernism, or the cultural logic of late capitalism* ushered in a new area in both Marxist and postmodern thought. Perhaps mostly influential is his thesis that postmodernism exists as more than simply a title for a specific historical period. Jameson (1991) counters this simplification using Marx's mode of production model to label postmodernism as a new social epoch within a capitalist schema, which, can be argued, moves it somewhat from the mode of production into the equally capitalist mode of consumption. This echoes the writings of Jean Baudrillard as a paradigmatic shift occurs in neo-Marxist writings changing from a production to a consumer determinant (Duvall, 1999). Jameson sees capitalism as having three distinct eras which carry a "cultural dominant" and he begins in the 19th century with what he refers to as the age of "market capitalism", also dubbed aesthetic realism. His second epoch begins in the early 20th century with "monopoly capitalism" as the cultural dominant; this is also seen as the modernist era. It serves to follow then that postmodernism would come next, and does, with what Jameson dubs "late capitalism".

He sees late capitalism as the multinational era in which we currently operate on a global scale, as opposed to what it is commonly referred to by others: the post industrial age (Kellner, 1997). While we are seeming to move from an industrial dominant in our culture, there is still a reliance on the industrial model to many extents in our societies. We are clearly not free of this dependence. Perhaps that is why Jameson eschews this term. His packaging of late capitalism thus accepts the industrial model as well as allowing newer technological and theoretical imperatives to exist as they are all able to simultaneously reside inside the conception of his cultural dominant. It is within this framework that Jameson expounds on his ideas of postmodern aestheticism which will be looked at in greater detail in chapter 3.

Linda Hutcheon's work on postmodernism emerges here, disagreeing with Jameson's approach to a certain extent, and taking some of his ideas further, politicizing them if you will. So while their views at times are conflicting and oppositional, I feel that it is both helpful and appropriate to utilize these views because as John Duvall (1999) explains, "Jameson's postmodernism focuses on the consumer, while Hutcheon's originates with the artist as producer" (p. 372). So while they often purport to be writing about the same thing, they have inherently different approaches to differing topics. Duvall explains this by showing how Jameson views the postmodern narrative as not having an historical reference as it simply uses a pastiche of imagery and aesthetic forms that at best presents history as degraded. Hutcheon meanwhile sees pastiche as missing the mark, at least historically. Rather than being ahistorical, pastiche is parody, an historical fiction that through the use of irony and satire serves to politicize history and serves as a cultural critique. At this point, a case study of an episode from The Simpsons is used to meld all elements into a singular cohesive that shows the relations inherent in these different ideals. It is this approach that will look at how The Simpsons creates a positive site for looking at aging.

The Simpsons began as a short skit on the *Tracy Ulman Show*, first introduced to the public on April 19, 1987 as one of 48 shorts (Hocking & Rose, 2003) that eventually aired. Series creator Matt Groening, a cartoonist and author of the alternative *Life in Hell* comic strip, claims that *The Simpsons* was his response to the shows he grew up watching. He has mentioned on more than one occasion that he was "strongly affected by 'Leave It to Beaver' and 'Ozzie and Harriet.' ['The Simpsons'] is my skewed reaction to those shows." (Mason, 1998). He also goes on to point out that the Simpsons are "a celebration of the American family at its wildest." Groening has also mentioned on more than one occasion that *The Simpsons* rewards its viewers for paying attention (Barney, 2003), and as the many fans will attest, due to its layers and textual density, gags, jokes, allusions, and subtle asides seem to emerge anew with each subsequent viewing. This dysfunctional family ultimately became the first prime time animated series since the 1960s (Todd, 2002) and the darling of the upstart Fox Network.

It was in the '60s that American television went through a short-lived animation boom. *The Flintstones* clearly set both the stage and the benchmark for other animated series to follow. Taking to the airwaves during the 1960 television season, Mittell (2003) points out how it took the recognized conventions of animation and virtually ignored them. This Hanna-Barbera creation and ABC television program sought an older audience by structuring the show like "a sitcom, complete with single half-hour episodes, suburban setting, domestic plots, and even a laugh track, deriving primary character and situational inspiration from *The Honeymooners*" (p. 45). As it turned out, the success of this program[3] led to a veritable onslaught of animated programming from the networks.

Following in the footsteps established by *The Flintstones*, such programs as *Top Cat* (ABC, 1961-62), *Calvin and the Colonel* (ABC, 1961-62), *The Alvin Show* (CBS, 1961-62), *The Jetsons* (ABC, 1962-63), *The Adventures of Jonny Quest* (ABC, 1964-65), and *The Famous Adventure of Mr. Magoo* (NBC, 1964-64) as well as a few other retooled or renamed animated series (Mittell, 2003). The success of *The Flintstones* is often attributed to the fact that while it was animated and thus appealed to younger children, it was also incredibly popular with teenaged audiences and even with adults. When *The Flintstones* was ultimately cancelled in 1966[4], it would be a full 23 years before *The Simpsons* would become the next prime time animated series with the first half hour episode appearing on the FOX network on December 17th, 1989.[5]

Debuting officially in 1990, *The Simpsons* was received with mixed reactions from many different sectors of society. It was hailed by many as a great social satire that

---

[3] It finished in 18th place in the overall Nielsen ratings for the season and remained in the top 30 for its first three seasons (Mittell, 2003). Nielsen TV ratings provide an estimate on the size of the audience for just about every program that can be seen on TV. (Nielsen media research)
[4] After being removed from the prime time schedule, *The Flintstones* lived in syndication on Saturday mornings and spun off a few other cartoons. (Rose, 2004).
[5] Although not officially the pilot episode (that was "Bart the Genius" which aired on January 14, 1990), or even the first episode produced (that was "Some Enchanted Evening" which didn't air until May 13, 1990), it was the first 30 minute episode to air on the Fox network. (Hocking & Rose, 2003).

attempted to show the flaws in our culture by scrutinizing familial relations, community, police, religion, politics, media, and our fascination with celebrity[6]. Others however mourned this apparent collapse in the family. In a now famous 1992 speech, ex-president George Bush lamented the "disintegration" of the American family and quipped to the effect that America needed families more like *The Waltons* and less like *The Simpsons*. This was addressed 3 days later on an episode of *The Simpsons*.

> **Ex-President Bush:** "We're going to keep trying to strengthen the American family. To make the American family a lot more like the Waltons and a lot less like the Simpsons."
>
> **Homer:** Huh?!?
>
> **Bart**: Hey, we're just like The Waltons. We're praying for an end to the depression, too! (Jean & Reiss, 1992, January 30)

As John Alberti (2004) writes, one of the reasons *The Simpsons* was so readily accepted by such a large number of viewers is the idea that since the show was seemingly so subversive, you often felt as though you were "getting away with something" (p. xii). This of course creates many questions, as well as a paradox of sorts. Can *The Simpsons* subvert something it seemingly embraces? While the content in the program often bemoans capitalism and the parasitic nature of celebrity, Simpsons products are for sale everywhere and characters from the show are clearly entrenched in popular culture, as is exemplified in the recent MasterCard ad with Homer that debuted in a coveted Super Bowl slot.

---

[6] In 1999, The Simpsons was hailed as the best TV program of the century by Time Magazine.

A recent study by The Annenberg Public Policy Center of the University of Pennsylvania found some interesting results. In the study the Center found that more American school children between the ages of 10 and 17 could identify Simpsons characters than could identify the then Vice-President of the United States, Al Gore (Al Gore vs. Bart Simpson, 2000). Ninety-Three percent of the children could accurately identify Simpsons characters while only sixty-three percent could identify the Vice-President. In Canada, a recent survey of children aged 8-15 accorded *The Simpsons* as the most popular show on television (Schmidt, 2003). While some have expressed concern over this by claiming that the subject material is for adults and not children, the director of the Center for the Study of Popular Television at Syracuse University, Robert Thompson, believes that parents should consider themselves lucky that their children are watching *The Simpsons*. As he states, the show is responsible for teaching children about such important topics as irony, political consciousness, and teaches them to approach media with a healthy scepticism (p. A13). Rather than ignoring or glossing over important social issues, *The Simpsons* has fore fronted and showcased important social concerns.

It is these issues that Savage (2004) points out as existing within *The Simpsons*, and as easy to identify. He suggests that in situations like this, as well as in shows like *South Park*, the writers have a tool to demonstrate, or at least hint, at how the audience should think about the cultural, political, or ideological content on the show. The device they use to indicate this is the cartoon within the cartoon, or in the case of *The Simpsons*, *The Itchy and Scratchy Show*. Savage sees this as an opportunity for the audience to see the serious nature of the program with regard to larger social issues and that despite its animated exterior and alleged status as children's programming, that their text can, and should, be read critically. Much like "novelists or playwrights include novels-within-novels or plays-within-plays in their works, sophisticated readers usually take that as an authorial hint regarding what (or how) to think about their medium" (p. 198). As anyone who has watched *The Simpsons* will attest, *The Itchy and Scratchy Show* does tackle important issues with its mocking satire, issue including violence, capitalism, and politics.

As Cantor (2001) notes, the show has tackled many important social issues over their tenure, including "nuclear power safety, environmentalism, immigration, gay rights, women in the military" and while a comedy, an often irreverent one at that, a paradox exists that "it is the farcical nature of the show that allows it to be serious in ways that many other television shows are not" (p. 161). The show has always served to polarize the public to varying degrees, and its format is largely responsible for that. What *The Simpsons* did was take the familiar conventions of the sitcom genre and rework them for a seemingly new twist. The twist was not entirely new, however, as it did draw from both the modern sitcom ideas as seen in *Roseanne*, but also paid (and continues to pay) a healthy tribute to *The Flintstones*. This is important to look at as it serves to counter one of Jameson's claim that parody is little more than an ahistorical pastiche.

Several instances have occurred in the history of *The Simpsons* that either directly reference *The Flintstones* or at the least allude to the modern stone aged family. At the beginning of every episode, the Simpson family make their way home from their individual activities. Bart rides his skateboard home from detention where he has been writing lines on the chalkboard, Lisa comes home on her bike after band practice, Marge and baby Maggie drive home after doing some grocery shopping, and Homer arrives at home after a hard day's work, well, a day's work at the local nuclear power plant. The family all arrive home at the same time and rush into the living room, leap onto the couch, and in perhaps the ultimate postmodern television moment, sit down to watch an episode of themselves on the TV. Each week, however, something new happens to the family as they head to the couch. At the beginning of the "Kamp Krusty" (Stern, D., 1992, September 24) episode, the Simpson clan head into the living room only to discover that Fred Flintstone, his wife Wilma and their daughter Pebbles are already sitting on the couch watching TV. There are other overt references as well.

While Homer is preparing to leave work in the episode "Marge Vs. the Monorail" (O'Brien, 1993, January 14), this homage to *The Flintstones* occurs:

> *As the Flintstones theme blares, Homer's slumber at his safety console is broken by the five o'clock whistle. With a Yabba-Dabba-Doo, Homer leaps into his car (crashing through the window) and speeds off. Song plays.*
>
> > Simpson! Homer Simpson!
> > He's the greatest guy in history.
> > From the, Town of Springfield!
> > He's about to hit a chestnut tree!
>
> *And he's right. Crash!*

The episode "Lady Bouvier's Lover" (Oakley & Weinstein, 1994, May 12) also features a direct reference to *The Flintstones*.

> *At the Simpson home, Marge walks down the stairs to join Homer.*

Marge: Mom's almost ready for her date. She sure seems taken by this new beau. I feel so bad for Grampa.

Homer: Dad says this new guy's a repulsive, obnoxious old billionaire. So let's all be extra-nice to him.

> [*doorbell rings; Homer answers it*]
> [*Marge and Homer scream*]

Burns: Hello! Why it's -- it's, er -- oh, it's er -- [*goes back, whispers to Smithers. Smithers whispers back and chuckles*] Why, it's Fred Flintstone and his lovely wife Wilma! Oh, and this must be little Pebbles. [*pats Maggie*] Mind if I come in? I've brought chocolates.

Homer: [*grabbing them*] Yabba dabba doo!

As Mullen (2004) points out, it is these types of tributes that "not only add to *The Simpsons's* (sic) extensive repertoire of inter-textual images, they also remind audiences of a rich tradition in television animation" (p. 64). So despite reworking the generic conventions of the situation comedy and animation, *The Simpsons* is still firmly rooted in the rich history these genres possess. This helps to counter Jameson by presenting the historicity to genre, convention, and textuality that he claims is missing. So while The Simpsons owe an historical, if not generic, debt to The Flintstones and other animated predecessors, in the context of this book, other programs need to be briefly acknowledged for their contributions to representations of the elderly on television.

When the topic of aging and television is broached, inevitably The Golden Girls are referenced. The Golden Girls was a popular and award winning program that ran from 1985-1992 and starred 4 older women who lived together in Florida (The Golden Girls, 2003). This show was important as it was one of the first programs that focused, not only entirely on female characters, but characters that could be identified as "older".

All of the actresses were about 60 years old when the program started and their characters were represented within the same age cohort as the actresses that portrayed them. Perhaps the most important feature of The Golden Girls was, as Harriet L. Cohen (2002) identified, that it allowed "viewers to see alternative images of older women on television and to question the existing sexist and ageist stereotypes" (p. 614). The BBC also ran a program from 1990-1994 titled Waiting for God that focused on the lives of elderly inhabitants of a British retirement home (Waiting for God, 2003). These are two of the limited examples of television programming that has focused on the elderly as main characters. The Simpsons, while not directly related to these programs per se, derive much historical meaning and generic convention from the field of animation.

Animated programming, relegated to Saturday mornings after the demise of the 1960s experiment, was unsurprisingly rejuvenated after the successes of *The Simpsons*. Many new animated programs emerged in prime time, with varying degrees of success. In the nineties a slew of shows emerged to capitalize on this apparent new boom. These included *The Critic*[7] featuring the voice of comedian Jon Lovitz, *Beavis & Butt-head, Ren & Stimpy, King of the Hill* and *Futurama* (both also on the Fox Network, *Futurama* also created by Groening), *South Park, Capitol Critters, Fish Police, Dr. Katz: Professional Therapist* and *Family Dog* to name a few of the new animated programs to show in prime time. Despite the success of *The Simpsons,* few of the new offerings were successful.

---

[7] *The Critic* was produced by James L. Brooks, also a producer for *The Simpsons.* In an act of synergy, the star of *The Critic*, New York film critic Jay Sherman, has appeared on *The Simpsons*

While it originally aired on the ABC television network, *The Critic* wouldn't last that long as it bounced around the network's line-up, sporadically making appearances here and there before ultimately being cancelled. Fox stepped in and picked up the series although this was short-lived and the series was ultimately cancelled (Hilton-Morrow & McMahan, 2003). In an obvious nod to new media and the direction entertainment may slowly be going, new, shorter episodes of *The Critic* are now broadcast online at www.atomfilms.shockwave.com. The other animated shows to debut after *The Simpsons* didn't last much longer, many despite their pedigrees.

While he had been extremely successful with television programming like *Hill Street Blues, L.A. Law, and NYPD Blue*, Steven Bochco had also failed miserably with his experimental *Cop Rock*. *Capitol Critters* would unfortunately follow in *Cop Rock's* footsteps. Based upon the lives of mice, rats, and roaches that lived in the White House, it only lasted one month before the exterminator was called in (Hilton-Morrow & McMahan, 2003). Likewise *Fish Police* only lasted 3 episodes, *Family Dog,* a Steven Spielberg and Tim Burton venture survived for one month, and with the exception of *South Park* and *King of the Hill*, none of these après-Simpson shows are still being produced for network consumption. *The Simpsons* thus occupy an important and unique area in television history.

Essentially from the beginning, the Fox Network knew it had a program on which to build a franchise, and they did. As the show picked up viewers and made its initial inroads onto the pop culture landscape, the network heads were already thinking big and planning ahead for the show. As Groening has said, "It was the beginning of the

Fox Network, and they were willing to take chances" (Simpsons broke new ground for cartoons, 2002, p. 26). Originally airing on Sunday nights (at this point in time the Fox Network was only presenting original programming on Saturdays, Sundays, and Mondays), Fox decided to move the surprise hit *The Simpsons* to an expanding schedule on Thursday nights, up against the reigning prime time sitcom, *The Cosby Show*. This move was made for a number of reasons. Firstly, it helped to solidify the notion of the Fox Network as the rebel, the outsider who was willing to go against the odds and take chances, and this was clearly a chance. Convention would say that a new show that was a surprise hit should not be moved from its successful time slot so soon, especially to confront the emperor (Goldman, 1990a). By doing just that, Fox showed that they laughed in the face of convention. But by this point, many were voicing their beliefs that *The Cosby Show* was losing steam and thus ripe for the picking. It was a gamble that would ultimately pay off for both *The Simpsons,* and the Fox network, but not right away.

Playing on their mystique as an irreverent newcomer, the network threw caution to the wind and moved *The Simpsons* to Thursdays against *The Cosby Show*, against the wishes of the producers of the animated family. Co-executive producer Sam Simon said at the time that "We were much more fragile than people thought, and I think it was much too soon to move us. But the show is important to everyone at Fox, so they won't let us die on Thursdays" (Goldman, 1990b) although it may have looked like it for a while. *The Cosby Show* took the first few shots, at least in the ratings, as they easily beat Homer and company. This prompted a *Cosby* co-executive producer to gloat somewhat as he publicly stated that the show may include an in joke involving *The Simpsons*. It was *The Simpsons,* however, that would get the last laugh.

By the halfway point in its second season, *The Simpsons* had essentially caught Cosby in the ratings, much to the delight of Fox heads who had resorted to free ad time after the initial poor showing against *The Cosby Show* (Fox's 'Simpsons' Closes In on NBC's 'Cosby' Ratings, 1990) . Ultimately, *The Cosby Show* was ready to be bested as its ratings dropped and the series started to become stale and repetitive. It was at this point that the writers for *The Simpsons* stole the Cosby thunder and incorporated an in joke of their own. Springfield family doctor Julius Hibbert was, and still is, a parody of the Bill Cosby character Dr. Heathcliff Huxtable. From his patterned sweaters to his characteristically over the top chuckle, it was clear from the outset who Dr. Hibbert was supposed to mirror. This use of parody would help to establish a linear connection with past historical TV referents, acknowledge the sitcom past, and ultimately look to a new future. Fox would move *The Simpsons* back to Sunday nights after vanquishing the Cosby clan, and with *King of the* Hill and the *X-Files*, change the television landscape again.

Sunday nights had long been a write off for regular networks. Save for *60 Minutes* and *Murder She Wrote* (which appealed to an entirely different, older demographic, one that at the time didn't appeal to advertisers), Sundays belonged almost solely to made for TV movies as other original programming stayed within the confines of the prime time weeknight block. Fox TV would use *The Simpsons* to rework that as well. Again, because of their postmodern aesthetics and historical parodic referents, *The*

Simpsons are able to achieve goals most regular programs cannot. While simultaneously referencing, twisting, and/or ignoring generic conventions, the show can achieve political goals unavailable to others shows and genres.

While other similar situation comedies like *All in the Family, M*A*S*H*, or Rosanne* occupied a similar role with its irreverent questioning of the status quo and overt social critiques, it can be argued that *The Simpsons* holds an advantage due to its form as an animated program. While the aforementioned shows inevitably grew stale and tired, *The Simpsons* is in its 21st season with no apparent sign of slowing down or becoming trite. *The Simpsons* managed to place 15th in the Nielsen ratings in only its 3rd month on the air and beating the popular *Murder She Wrote* on CBS (Bauder, 2004). As recently as September 2009, *The Simpsons,* beginning their 21st season, still placed 15th in the coveted 18-49 adult demographic. There a few programs in the history of television with both the staying power and unwavering popularity that *The Simpsons* has shown as it has just surpassed *Gunsmoke* as the longest running primetime show on American television. As Alberti (2004) argues,

> Not bounded by the physical laws governing 3-D space, animated programs can feature casts of hundreds and take place in any geographic or historical time frame. In the case of the animated prime time television series, this "cartoon for grown-ups" inhabits a cultural space between children's programming and prime time programming. This ambiguous cultural space allows producers and writers to take advantage of the resulting uncertainty regarding generic expectations from this mixing of the childlike and the adult, the supposedly trivial and the serious, by being able to treat serious and even controversial issues under the cover of "just being a cartoon". (p. xiii)

Just being a "cartoon" may give *The Simpsons* a distinct advantage in being truly critical and oppositional.

As past television theorists like Horace Newcomb (2000) and others have noted, TV and TV aesthetics are art as they present a narrative format that is used to explain or alert viewers to a larger social reality. Genre was paramount in this ideal as it was responsible for how meaning and ideology resided within format and also how it was presented. As such, the structures of modern television were somewhat defined and static, repeatable and inherently predictable. With the emergence of The Simpsons and its postmodern aesthetic and redefined as well as reconfigured notions of generic convention, it allows for it to operate in a manner that few other programs can. The Simpsons "is hyperreal, it gestures first and foremost to itself" (Ott, 2003, p. 60) and herein lies its true power. It reworks our social and cultural space by allowing for a critique of what we see as 'natural', as will be demonstrated in this book. It is this cultural space within which the Simpson family resides and within which they address the questions and issues they do, including ideas of aging.

AGING STUDIES

Dr. Hibbert delivers a speech at the opening of the Springfield Center for Geriatric Medicine.

Hibbert: Er, welcome to the new Springfield Center for Geriatric Medicine. You know, health care for the aging is an important priority in this –

Abe: Get to Matlock! Maaatlooock!

Hibbert: Well, uh, ahem, without further ado, heh heh, I give you the man who puts young people behind bars -- where they belong. TV's Matlock!
[An old man with two canes walks slowly onto the stage]

Crowd: *[singing]* We love you Matlock, oh yes we do...

In their excitement, the crowd turns violent and rushes the stage, knocking poor Matlock over and tugging cruelly at his collar, tearing it. Someone even puts their cane around his throat.
(Oakley & Weinstein, 1994, February 17)

Aging & the Media

Currently, all of North America is undergoing rapid change in its distribution of age. A shift is taking place that is seeing our population age which is creating a situation where social institutions are having to deal with new and emerging issues. With advances in the fields of medicine, technology, and other sciences, people are living longer than they ever have before. The addition to this equation of dropping fertility rates is responsible for this increase of aged in our population. It is these issues that are creating concerns in many different and diverse sectors of society. Pensions, health care, housing issues, and welfare are under increasing scrutiny as our aging population is appearing to put demands on them that cannot be sustained. Before any of these issues and concerns can be adequately addressed, however, we need to understand, as a society, what our preconceived notions of aging are and what they entail. Mass media have managed to transmit countless impressions of the elderly that have shaped an ideology towards aging that many of us carry. Countless studies in recent years have shown how media portrayals of the elderly have started to change, but how much have they changed, why have they changed, and what purpose is served by this transformation in imagery?

As a technology, TV has stepped up in the past half century to reach for the mantle as the most pervasive cultural medium in history. Rapidly advancing communications technologies have brought us closer to Marshall McLuhan's notion of the global village, and television is but one of the tools employed in this cultural and economic globalization. Music, print media, radio, theatre (live and cinematic), web based entertainment and the Internet also serve in the transmission of these ideological messages to the masses.

A veritable wealth of research has been conducted into how the mass media has primarily presented images of aging. It has effectively served to present the elderly as frail, dependent, senile, and as non-productive members who place undue strain on the larger social system. With these continual images bombarding consumers worldwide, a group that is viewed by many as socially irrelevant and burdensome has been successfully moved to the margins of society. The interesting thing to note in this scenario is that it differs greatly from how the elderly see themselves.

In the existing literature, there are many factors that influence the approach taken, and the results affected. The disciplinary background of the researcher, the ultimate goals of the study, who has financed the research, or the source materials used can all affect how aging is studied and defined. Aging in and of itself poses a problem globally in that it means many things to many people. Culture, age, and life experience are all factors that affect how one views aging in their society, or in their life. According to the texts, however, there are four major ways in which to define aging for research.

Aging is seen as a chronological progression through the life course. Barry McPherson (1998) defines chronological aging as a legal tool and an "approximate indicator" of the different social and physical developments one faces; it is not always a defining measure in the idea of aging (p. 11). This is but one of the components that McPherson identifies as integral to research into aging. He also identifies biological, psychological, and social components to the aging process.

Biological aging is defined as characterized by the internal and external changes that occur in the human body. These include things such as greying of hair or wrinkles developing in the skin. Psychological aging is referent to one's personality, including memory, creativity, behaviour, and any changes that may occur in these. According to McPherson (1998), these are usually borne out in certain events like having to adapt to new surroundings or major events that "affect our psychological state" (p. 11).

Social aging is essentially how the elderly are viewed in their society. McPherson writes, "values and norms may determine whether elderly people experience loneliness and abandonment, or whether they are supported and integrated into society" (p.12). This is reflected with the interaction that exists between the aging person and society. Some social institutions exclude the elderly, while other cultures may include or even exalt aging. The segmentation or division of society along age lines may also preclude the voice or experience of the elderly individual. While biological and psychological aging remain essentially constant across cultures, it is social aging which differs most. Aging is thus an incredibly complex and diverse process that incorporates aspects of physiology, psychology, sociology, and gerontology in an attempt to explain all the different phenomenon that can affect a person over their life course.

One of the most important notes that can be taken from all the differing research is that different studies employ different measures when looking at age. Even if it appears on the surface that two different studies are researching the same thing, it is often the case that differing criteria or operational definitions are employed that can ultimately affect what is presented. So while much of the research purports to tell the same story, they often offer different results or opinions based on the criteria used. For example, Robinson and Skill (1995) looked at portrayals of the elderly on prime time television and used the age of 65 as their measure. Markson and Taylor (2000), however, used the age of 60 in their research looking at the portrayal of the aged in motion pictures. Nancy Signorielli (2001) used a double-barrelled approach to aging by using a chronological guideline and adding a social age component[8] in her look at the representation of the elderly on television. Three different studies, all essentially looking for the same measure are using different guidelines and thus offer differing results or percentages based on their choices.

---

[8] "Social age" includes a guess at a character's chronological age while utilizing social tools to help gauge age. These tools include "the perspectives of stages on the life-cycle. Social age isolates characters who are children or adolescents, young adults, settled or middle-aged adults (those who have steady employment, a family, for example), and older people" (2001, p.35) Using this in conjunction with textual clues such as retirement, age of family or children would be used to help identify those characters believed to be at least 60 years old.

This shows how imperative it is to have a clearly defined operationalization for age, and to remain cognizant of how these definitions are used in other research.

Our population is aging according to the latest results from the Canadian census, and shows no signs of abating; in fact, predictions are that population aging will continue to increase. According to the 1996 results, 12 per cent of the country's 30 million citizens were over the age of 65 (Martin-Matthews, 1999). The 2001 census shows the continuation of this trend as represented in table 1. In this report, 12.7 per cent of the 31.4 million citizens were over the age of 65 (Statistics Canada, 2001). This is expected to reach almost 15 per cent by 2011 (Statistics Canada, 2002). Canada's median age reached an all time high of 37.6 years which is an increase of 2.3 years from its number of 35.3 in 1996 (Statistics Canada, 2001). This was recognized as the single largest census increase in the past century. The trend towards aging increased with the census report that the population aged 80 or older increased by 41.2 per cent. Projections are for a further increase of 43 per cent in the next decade as shown in table 1.

Table 1 - Median age, Canada, 1901-2011

	Median age
1901	22.7
1911	23.8
1921	23.9
1931	24.7
1941	27.0
1951	27.7
1956	27.2
1961	26.3
1966	25.4
1971	26.2
1976	27.8
1981	29.6
1986	31.6
1991	33.5
1996	35.3
2001	37.6
2006	39.5
2011	41.0

Table 1. Statistics Canada

Factor in the decreasing fertility rates and these trends should continue. It is important to notice how the population actually exists in our society, how it is dispersed, and how it is changing before noting how it is represented in the mass media.

Representations

The politics of representation are vast and traverse many disciplines and fields of thought. Race, gender, and age are but a few of the cultural discourses that are garnering attention in media studies. As Julie D'Acci (2004) points out,

> if television is a term with multiple meanings and is currently caught up in revolutionary changes (many the result of technological and geopolitical shifts), "representation" too has many meanings and is itself undergoing conceptual transformations. Recently, a number of philosophical and theoretical debates, as well as scientific advances (in, for example, the field of physics) have revolved around the notion of representation and its presumed correlate, reality." (p. 374)

As she later explains, we have this notion that what we see on TV is a reflection of reality, that a mirror has been held up to our world and is being shown back to us on the television. This however may be too simplistic of a look at how television represents our realities.

As she continues to expand on the question of television representations, D'Acci believes that television is simply a mediator between the human and that outside of the human, essentially a socially constructed "reality" that serves as a proxy of sorts for a reality that may or may not exist in a larger truth about nature and human existence. As we have seen in the world of television recently with questions abounding around the world of "reality" television, the reality is in fact, not reality at all.

With camera shots retaken, cast members re-shooting scenes that are presented on the program as live or off the cuff, extras being used to redo a scene well after the fact, or vignettes pre-recorded and inserted into scenes that have no correlate to each other, reality television is in fact not real at all. It has been said that the camera never lies, but in fact the camera never tells the truth. At least not the whole truth. By taking a situation and condensing it into a framed shot, it excludes the world outside of the frame, selectively presenting what the photographer wants shown. It also removes the context of the occurrence, leaving a contextual blank slate which is open to many different interpretations. It is this selectiveness which problematizes the representations of the elderly. What is the impetus for what is shown, for how a group of people are presented? Whether it is economic, political, or some other social force, it is problematic for the group being shown.

This can create a situation which Michel Foucault called a "regime of truth" (Hall, 1997). In this occurrence, an absolute truth is not only false but irrelevant. If something is believed to be true, it has a real affect on our social sphere. If from watching representations of elderly people on TV we come to see all older individuals as infirmed or a drain on social resources, while this is clearly not supportable in any way, it becomes a discursive reality in the respect that many believe it to be true, creating a regime of truth. We can see this at work in representations of the elderly.

In the majority of the research produced about aging in the mass media, especially it would seem in North American research, the elderly are under represented in proportion to the actual numbers they have in the larger population (Evers, 1998). It should be noted that looking beyond "simply" studying aging, a great deal of the research also addresses questions of gender and race. The history of media research into elderly and the media, particularly television is a relatively new endeavour.

According to Healey and Ross (2002), studies were conducted that looked at television as early as the 1950s, but it wasn't until the 70s that that the first substantial look at television was truly conducted using more comprehensive content analyses. It was during this era of research that an alarming picture emerged which showed the elderly as under represented and negatively portrayed on the small screen (Mares & Cantor, 1992).

According to the research, negative depictions of the elderly take many different forms. Most of the researchers agree that the media tends to portray elderly people as frail, lonely, in financial distress, as non-productive, or socially redundant (Evers, 1998; Featherstone & Hepworth, 1995; Featherstone & Wernick, 1995; Hareven, 1995; McPherson, 1998). All point to the popular societal myths that tend to exaggerate or magnify smaller truths and occur with an alarming regularity in the mass media. It is these negative stereotypes that help to create a negative stigma with aging. While it is true that some elderly people may require varying levels of care or assistance, with the media framing the elderly as a "social problem" or as a group with "special needs" (Weaver, 1999, p. 487), a negative connotation to the elderly is formed. Susan Feldman (1999) notes in her essay that "contrary to negative views about growing old, the reality for most people is that ageing can be characterised by relatively good health, activity and independence" (p. 270). These negative stereotypes do not work alone, however.

In conjunction with other societal representations, these stereotypes help to promote and perpetuate existing social ideology about age and aging (Markson & Taylor, 2000). There is often a sinister element as well as Evers (1998) notes that these stereotypes "are frequently employed in order to justify discrimination against minorities" (p.12). The question, of course, remains as to whether the media help to create this negative ideology or whether they simply mirror it, although it is important to recognize that regardless of motives or intentions, these negative images of aging are detrimental to a group of marginalized individuals (Harwood, 2000).

Consider that in TV's *Image of the Elderly*, authors Davis and Davis (1985) advance some informative research findings into the representation of the elderly by pointing out that based on their research and the research of others that "it is obvious that the numbers of older people appearing on television do not correlate with the numbers of older people in society" (p. 45). They point out that while TV is not supposed to be a realistic portrayal of everyday life, the absence, or in this case limited exposure, of a group helps to make them appear trivial or unimportant. They argue that simply by virtue of appearing on a television screen, a group or individual "becomes important" (p. 45) and by extension, their absence denotes that they are unimportant.

As many of the studies concluded, "the negative portrayals of older people impact on the ways in which older people are perceived by their community at large" (Healey & Ross, 2002, p. 110). As a recognized agent of socialization, the mass media have served to transmit social values and ideals. This transmission of negative aging imagery has helped to indoctrinate a generation or more to the ideology that being elderly is abnormal. Popular culture conveys the message that youth is desirable and the ultimate goal to obtain, which serves to devalue the elderly in our society by representing them with little or no social value. This creates the ideology that even as we age, we must strive to maintain the ideals of youth in both physical appearance and attitude.

By presenting this image of youth as the social norm, the opposite end of the life course—where the elderly reside—is by default abnormal (Lock, 1993). This is best exemplified in Western culture by the copious amounts of advertising that promises to mask signs of aging, or to put the entire process into arrest, all of this obviously available with the purchase of a consumer good (Markson & Taylor, 2000). It is these falsehoods and age related ideologies that we carry into our everyday lives, ultimately affecting our perceptions in a generally negative manner.

Robinson and Skill, in their study on the portrayal of the elderly on prime time TV concluded that characters aged 65 or older are "an invisible generation on television" (1995, p.111). A random sample of 100 prime time American TV programs was measured and they found that only 2.8 per cent of the adult characters were identified as being at least 65 years old. As this study would have been undertaken in approximately 1994, about 1 in 8 Americans was actually aged 65 or older (US Census Bureau, 1994). Despite the fact that the American population over age 65 actually constituted nearly 12 per cent of the total population, they only made up 2.8 per cent of the prime time TV population. The majority of the research conducted in the 70s and 80s also supported this conclusion as most show this group representing less than 5 per cent of the TV population (p.111). Studies conducted after this one have reached similar results.

Nancy Signorielli's (2001) study concluded that only 3 per cent of the prime time characters on US network television could ultimately be characterized as elderly. She studies a sample consisting of twelve weeks of programming including sitcoms, dramas, action-adventure, magazine style programs, and reality shows to reach her conclusions. She also noted that beyond the blanket 3 per cent representation of elderly characters, men outnumber women 6-4 and the largest group represented is middle-aged. She attributes this distribution as "representative of groups who have more disposable income" (p. 35). She also notes how the imagery of aging was constructed in the programs. She found that of those deemed over the age of 65, only 75 per cent of the men were socially constructed as elderly while 83 per cent of the women were. She thus concludes that there exists a major disjunction between television messages regarding aging versus the reality that most experience in their lives. In this field of research, however, television is not the only culprit.

Investigating to see if motion pictures conveyed an accurate reflection of the elderly population, Markson and Taylor (2000) looked at this medium as they note it "has been a powerful tool to deliver both explicit and implicit messages about appropriate behaviour and attitudes" (p. 139). Their measure was characters aged 60 and over and they looked to see if the reality of this social cohort was accurately reflected on the big screen. They ultimately concluded that while the social role and daily activities of this age group has undergone an incredible shift since the 1930's, the same could not be said for the portrayals of this group in films. They note that the stereotyping and imagery projected on the screen includes those used to "connect the visible, physical changes associated with aging to built-in obsolescence and physical and mental decay" (p. 144). This theme is noted in other research as well (Feldman, 1999; Gerbner, Gross, Signorielli, & Morgan, 1980) although few can agree on the levels to which it exists. In a study conducted in 1973, Peterson found that "as many as 13 per cent of the characters on TV were 65 or older (1973; cited in Robinson & Skill, 1995, p. 111). While most research acknowledges the Peterson study, it is clearly identified as an anomaly in the field and is questioned for its ambiguous techniques and measures.

The music industry has also been examined for its images of aging. A study conducted by Aday and Austin (2000) looks at American country music to see how elderly persons are lyrically portrayed. They chose this area as they felt it "plays an important role in our society, and its lyrics often deal with real concerns and problems of America and its people" and as a "powerful component of cultural norms" (p.136). They chose 52 songs that spanned over 45 years and all had received a modicum of public exposure. They concluded that the lyrics in country music contained more negative images related to aging than it did of positive ones. The elderly were represented in the lyrics that focused on "physical and mental attributes, mobility and reaction time, and loneliness and isolation were found to be negative in nature" (p. 150). The one major exception to this rule was when the elder in question was looked at as a parent or grandparent, in which case the image created was more positive.

The print media was also looked at and didn't fare much better. A random sample of 5000 articles from European magazines and newspapers was only able to produce a total of 20 articles which "appear to refer to older people" (NPOE, 1996, p.5; as cited in Evers, 1998, p.14). In addition to this gross under representation, the study's authors found that when they did appear in an article, the elderly were constructed as a social problem and a financial expense. There is also research that identifies an emerging breed of positive imagery around aging that needs to be addressed here.

In the past 30 years, some of the negative images surrounding the elderly have been slowly moving from the stereotypical negative portrayals to a new, marketing based discourse that deals in more positive images. These new images of aging are not being created or transmitted for any larger social good, however, they are tied directly to the economic ideal of consumption. Despite the fact that audiences perceive an improvement in the images of aging shown on television, Robinson and Skill (1995) report that they could find no evidence to support that claim. Their research showed fewer visible elderly on TV in the early '90s than in the '70s, and the roles they occupied were not substantially removed from their predecessors. They believe that an increase in "older", but not necessarily elderly characters was a reason for this confusion. It is important to note that in the 1990s, an increase was recorded in the portrayal of older characters (Robinson & Skill, 1995), even if they were not codified as elderly. This seemingly shows that marketers were following a specific cohort of consumers, namely the baby boomers, and targeting a wide array of advertising and programming at them as they progressed through their life course. In fact, a study by Dail concluded that television media realised that the aging population in the US had considerable power, economically and politically (1988).

Marketers realise this as a potential market niche, as exemplified in this article from the *International Journal of Market Research* where author Rizal Ahmad (2002) writes:

> The realities of the consumer market in the UK are that: the number and the proportion of older population/ageing consumers are growing; older consumers have substantial buying power for certain products and services; and they have high levels of expectation. Older consumers also do not associate their consumption behaviours with their chronological ages. Instead, they behave like many young people. (p. 357).

While this marketing study was conducted on individuals from the United Kingdom, there is no reason to think that the results would be any different in North America. In fact, we see this ideal reflected on TV.

Television essentially serves one purpose, to deliver the largest consumer audience possible to a proliferation of advertisers. Those forty minutes of every television hour are only there to attract specific markets to the altar of consumption. Media, as with most every aspect of modern life, is increasingly just about products. As Markson and Taylor so eloquently state, "during the 20th century, the work ethic of early capitalist culture has transformed into a consumer culture—from 'I am what hard work I do' to 'I am what I can buy'" (2000, p. 138). It is this marketing driven view that has helped to create increasingly positive images of aging.

With consumers over the age of 50 controlling half of the discretionary income in North America (Sawchuk, 1995), new marketing techniques are looking to dispel the negative discourse that exists around aging. This shift has seen individuals who were once de-commodified at retirement, re-commodified as an attractive consumer market (Tulle-Winton, 1999). As advertising has managed to segregate society into small measurable segments of consumers, the elderly find themselves looking at positive images of aging that are created to tap into a newly recognized and lucrative piece of the market. As Sawchuk writes, while the old strategies have created and perpetuated myths about the elderly, new positive images of aging are creating new ones as the focus is solely on commodification of the aging body (1995). Advertisers have followed the lucrative baby boomers over their life span, and are realizing that our aging population is also a generally wealthy population.

There have been studies conducted as well that find an alleged middle ground between under representation and positive portrayals. Research conducted by Roy and Harwood (1996) investigated the content of 778 American television commercials. They acknowledged that the elderly had primarily been stereotyped or ignored in the media until recently. Marketers had a growing awareness of the purchasing power possessed by the older generations, and as such a paradigmatic shift was taking place. They concluded that while the elderly were under represented in the population of these 778 TV commercials, the portrayals that they received were essentially positive in nature. They were in fact a heavily recognized demographic in advertisements that focused on finances and the retail chains which showed them as "strong, happy, and active" (p. 51). This shows the marketers' increasing desire of the aging demographic and its changing position in the consumer arena. Interestingly, they note that a "small number of positive portrayals may represent advertisers' desire not to alienate older consumers" (p. 51). It is the recognition of this market's attractiveness to advertisers that is important to note. While social scientists and gerontologists may have been the first to call for more positive images of aging in the media, it was the advertiser who finally heeded the call. While overcoming the "devalued and feared" representations of the aged body (Tulle-Winton, 1999), marketers have created a discourse on successfully aging. Rather than promoting positive images of the elderly simply to overcome the myths and negative stereotypes however, positive images are increasing in their frequency, but are tied to the ideal of youth, and tied to consumption of a commercial good. Examples of this are Oil of Olay to remove wrinkles; literally thousands of vitamins and nutritional supplements that claim to stop aging, and health care services are also promising to deliver successful aging with treatments like laser surgery, plastic surgery, and hormone therapy treatments.

So these products and millions like them, bring more positive images of being elderly into the marketplace and onto our TV screens, but they do not represent the real lives or concerns of the aged. By focusing on the elderly as a target market in the need of products, only a small percentage of these elderly are able to participate, and thus represented. If a senior does not have the financial resources to participate in the market economy, then they are left as invisible on the margins of society. Positive images in mass media are used primarily to generate sales, not to recognize or address any of the specialized needs that may exist in the older community. It could be argued that for those groups unable to take part in consumer culture, there does not exist much positive imagery of their aging. If their market cannot be mined for considerable financial gain, then they are unattractive and invisible to marketers. Also, the voice being used is not their own, it belongs to someone with an agenda other than realistically portraying another's lived experiences and surely that has to be seen as problematic. So while the majority of the research shows that media images are generally stereotypical and negatively framed, except when targeting the elderly as a specific consumer group, the elderly themselves have an entirely different conception of their aging selves.

Self Conception/Identity

Identity in modern society seems more complex and harder to define than ever before. With the opportunity for individuals to have membership in many different and diverse groups, it would seem that the idea of a "single fixed identity" is no longer a viable construct to consider. As we attempt to define ourselves in relation to the multiple activities and components of our lives, it would appear that a multifaceted approach to the politics of individual and social identities needs to be employed. Can this be achieved through a piecemeal approach to existing theoretical frameworks in the area, or does a new school of thought need to emerge to answer these questions? Perhaps more importantly, how do current theories of identity apply to the elderly individual? Identity and age may offer even more variables and thus a tougher question is potentially posed. Does media representation of the aging individual influence elderly identity? The politics of identity are fraught with opposing ideas and contradictions, but it is imperative to sketch some historical glimpse into the area before moving more directly into the relationship to aging.

Craig Calhoun (1994) has also identified what he sees as an historical basis for the evolution of identity theories, and it is their flexibility and malleability that give these theories credence and acceptance, not their rigidity. Calhoun sees early social theory and identity concerns as focusing on individuals as singular unique entities unto themselves and to that end ignored difference between people. If you focus on one person or individual at the exclusion of all others, then comparison or difference cannot be utilized as a tool of reflection. Early individual identity was directly linked to the legal acceptance of ownership and property rights as entitlement to inclusion in the social and political spheres. As time began to erode these ideas of citizenry and ultimately of identity, a new school of thought emerged that considered a new set of circumstances in social life. It was with this new theory that a new social self emerged, one tied to the changes that society was undergoing, and in the process would seek to redefine what identity was, in a micro and a macro environment. As Calhoun (1994) points out, identity is based on many theories that:

> underestimate the struggle involved in forging identities, the tension inherent in the fact that we all have multiple, incomplete and/or fragmented identities (and sometimes resistances), the politics implied by the differential public standing of various identities or identity claims, and the possibilities for our salient constructions of identities to change in the context of powerfully meaningful, emotionally significant events. (p. 24)

Calhoun even goes a step further as he identifies identity theories as essentially interchangeable due to increasing relativist thought and an influx of postmodern scholarship. This pastiche of theory is essential in this situation as the complexity of identity and the multiplicity of responsibilities ensures that different areas of an individual's identity politics are addressed.

In their thorough and seemingly comprehensive look at issues of identity, Holstein and Gubrium (2000) chart a linear map through a history of identity theorizing. Their evaluation of the theories begin with William James, Charles Horton Cooley, and George Herbert Mead. While acknowledging that questions of self and identity were raised during the Enlightenment, it was the pragmatists who broke with the philosophical self presented in the transcendental musings of Descartes and Rousseau. Yet, it was the common everyday approach of James that set a new empirical bar for future looks at identity. He distinguished between the "I" and the "me" portions of identity that allow us to objectify ourselves. Holstein and Gubrium also believe that James set forth the notion "that when we communicate with others about who we are, we again inadvertently convey both subjectivity and objectivity" (p. 23). It was these ideas of social interaction that were taken up by later theorists.

Holstein and Gubrium also look at the looking glass self of Cooley as "rooted in self-feeling" and that it "operates in the imagination, drawing from, reflecting upon, and responding to real and imagined others" (p.27). Although there is an intrinsically instinctive ideal in Cooley's model, Mead manages to remove instinct and initiate a more socially interactive model. While also employing an "I" and "me" naming scheme, Mead makes a pointed differentiation by heavily distinguishing the interactional and social elements in his construct. To Mead, there is no self without interaction. It is "part of the process of communication…it doesn't exist before it, nor does it develop and come to be expressed through it" (p. 29).

Mead (1934) writes that the self is an ongoing social experience that arises from interaction in the social sphere, and we are not limited to only one idea of "self". He writes that:

> We are one thing to one man and another thing to another. These are parts of the self which exist only for the self in relation to itself. We divide ourselves up in all sorts of different selves with reference to our acquaintances. We discuss politics with one and religion with another. There are all sorts of different selves answering to all sorts of different social reaction. It is the social process itself that is responsible for the appearance of the self; it is not there as a self apart from this type of existence. (p. 142)

It is both the social nature, and the multiplicity of self that are important to remember in the context of this book.

It is our interaction and social ties that many feel provide the anchor for who we are. It is these links to others that offer notions of self, according to Auger and Tedford-Litle (2002). Our participation in society entitles us to "membership in and interactions with social groups such as family, friends, neighbourhood, community, and the various activities in which we engage" (p. 107). For elderly individuals, this sense of membership is believed to be a critical component of positive aging. A positive attitude and feeling of belonging is crucial in fostering a sense of self-worth directly correlated to our social interaction. "We are social beings who bring to our interactions expectations, beliefs, and feelings about others and ourselves" (p. 107). It is the inclusion of our feelings about others that stand out here.

This plays back into Mead's notion of reflection. If we envision ourselves as others see us, then from this must emerge the rules and protocols we associate with our image of self. This is where certain representations become important. Owens and Goodney (2000) make the connection to a larger social relation of self. They write that:

> since the self emerges from social interaction, it reflects the qualities and the structures of the society where the interaction occurs. Consequently, if one wants to investigate the self in a given society, one must be prepared to ultimately grapple with the nature and structure of the society (p. 38).

As such, society and self are intrinsically linked, and this is where representation and other social concerns become problematic.

If others see a person as old and useless because they have seen them characterized that way on TV, this reflects onto the elderly individual themselves through social interaction. Now, while this person may not see themselves as the other sees them, according to Mead's theory, these stereotypes do in fact become a part of that older individual's identity make-up. They hold these feelings as being true or appropriate for others whereas they negate that these same terms apply to themselves. "It is for this reason that older persons share the same stereotypes about their generation" (Auger & Tedford-Litle, 2002, p. 109).

As has been demonstrated through existing literature and within the emergent methodological approach of the qualitative model, identity theory is vast and differing. The lack of a definitive theory to explain all questions of identity and self-perception indicates that a mosaic approach must be undertaken. Society is a constantly evolving entity, changing over time and adapting to new sets of questions, providing us with different answers, and even more emerging questions. As we undergo change at a larger social level, we as individuals are also trying to find out how we are positioned within this schema; where we are in relation to larger societal forces.

Ethnographies into the thoughts and perceptions of the elderly have demonstrated that while they are presented a primarily negative picture of aging in the mass media, their impressions of themselves are altogether different. This style of research and the use of storytelling allows for the voices of those on the margins of society to be heard. When listening to the voices of the persons being investigated, one is able to overcome the sterility associated with the more quantitative approaches to research which "emphasize numerical precision; a detached, aloof stance on the researcher's part" (Palys, 1997, p. 423). By allowing for the voice to be heard, many barriers can be broken down or disassembled including the idea of the "Other" that occurs in Western society when looking at the elderly, both male and female (Dossa, 1999, p. 246). The "Other" implies that the values and standards of the researcher have been applied to the researched, effectively changing or denying their voice (in this case elderly people) in how they understand their own experiences subjective to their own lived existence (Palys, 1997). Granting a voice to the elderly allows them to finally speak for themselves and can help to realise a more balanced power relation within the larger social structure.

There is slowly beginning to emerge new research that does just that. This approach ultimately allows the elderly a social forum with which to relate how they see the media images of aging in relation to how they perceive their own social being against this media created backdrop. Interestingly, it seems to be advertisers and marketers that took the first foray into this field as they looked to develop new methods and techniques to tap into this lucrative financial market.

Bradley and Longino (2001) conducted a study to see how elderly consumers saw others their age, how they see the concept of aging, and how they see themselves amidst this sea of images presented in the media and through advertising. The results of this research showed that to the elderly, "age is not very central in defining who older people think they are" (p. 17). They looked back at studies conducted a generation earlier and saw that as Americans aged, they saw the notions of health, income, loneliness, and crime as less of an issue for themselves than the younger respondents felt it would be in their old age. Their hypotheses then was that the negative imagery of aging stems from the fact our culture promotes beauty and the aging body is not seen as beautiful by these standards. Countless others researchers and social scientists seem to support this scenario (Bytheway, 1993, as cited in Bradley and Longino, 2001; Chaney, 1995; Lock, 1993).

The "denial of aging" theory (Bultena & Powers, 1979) states that when asked to identify themselves within a scheme that defines how they see their own age, the elderly tend not to see themselves as old. When given the opportunity to place themselves on a continuum of differing age related categories, most people judge themselves as chronologically younger than they are. Recent research from sociolinguists, among other disciplines, have focused on "the meaning behind such age identifying or disidentifying statements", even though the authors realise this is only "one way of broaching the task of investigating people's self-concepts in old age" (Coupland, Coupland, & Giles, 1991, p.56-57). The authors also identify aging and identity as placed within a social constructivist approach, firmly entrenching it within the qualitative method.

They identify elderly identity as constantly changing and unstable, "reflecting the local circumstances in which it is produced" (p. 56). It is the local component that recognizes the inherent subjectivity of the individual, as they construct their own identities within a community. A discursive analysis of elder talk shows that the theme of "elderliness" indicates the elderly identify themselves by denying aging.

In their research, Mares and Cantor (1992) found the results "indicate that people respond differently to portrayals of old age, depending on their prior preoccupations" (p. 473). Essentially they concluded that a negative portrayal, as in that of a lonely elder, could make a lonely elder feel better about themselves by internalizing that perhaps they are not so bad off after all, at least compared to that image. Conversely, a happy image could make that elder feel even worse about themselves…or vice versa. So if, as the research seems to indicate, the media conveys negative images of the elderly, should not the elderly see themselves as well off, at least compared to the negative images they see of their cohorts?

Research conducted by Natalie Rosel (2001) indicates that one learns to play roles over the course of their entire life, and even as one ages, we model ourselves after images that are deemed relevant to ourselves. She sums up this thought by stating that "we see images or models in relation to how we see ourselves" (p. 47). Where this creates a problem, however, is exemplified in her research which looks at how rural elders read media images and concluded that they were not offered any relevant role models from the media they saw. She travelled to a rural village in Maine and interviewed its elderly inhabitants over a four month period. She noted that they referenced the print media more than TV or radio when discussing the media, and none of the respondents even had a television on when she arrived for an interview. The interesting idea to emerge from this is the notion many hold that the elderly and children are the largest audiences for TV programming (Signorielli, 2001). Rosel's findings are supported, at least in theory, by Statistics Canada (TV…, 2002) which report that while the total population averages 21.5 hours of television viewing in a week, children (2-11) watched only 15.5 hours and adolescents (12-17) watched only 14.1 hours of TV per week; the lowest total of any group. Although the elderly are not specifically listed as a separate entity in this report, other research supports the argument that older individuals are not the heavy TV consumers many believe (Healey & Ross, 2002). The roles we take are modeled after imagery that the individual has deemed relevant to their situation.

Environment may also play a focal role in how the elderly consume different media. Rosel's study shows that in a rural aging in place scenario, the TV may not be used for much more than "the purpose of hearing another voice in the house" (p. 49). This seemingly makes the connection between media consumption and environment, as the rural elders appear to have different consumptive patterns from their urban counterparts. Evers (1998) offers a Dutch survey that shows the elderly see television as an important component of their lives. It is more than just a medium for entertainment as they use it to stay up to date with what is happening all over the world. As a vehicle of entertainment however, many elderly feel that is the least important of its functions as it is used primarily for "news and current affairs" programming (p. 20). So while the television may play an important feature for the elderly, it is not necessarily for entertainment but information.

A study conducted by Hofstetter and Schultze (1993) set out to determine if the elderly who watch TV perceive negative stereotyping based on age and are the negative stereotypes based more in chronological age or a contextual aging schema dependent on biological, psychological, and social components. A sample of elders aged 55 and over was conducted in which the respondents were further stratified according to age. In total 593 people were interviewed via the telephone in 1989. The researchers concluded that the majority of the TV viewers interviewed felt the elderly were portrayed in a favourable manner on TV. Perhaps the most important aspect to this research, however, was the finding that as the respondent's age increased, they became more aware of stereotypical representations and negative representations on TV.

Healey and Ross (2002) also undertook a case study of older television viewers. One of the salient points to emerge from this research is that the elderly are fully aware of the perceptions others hold toward them. A few of the responses regarding this included "They think if you're old, you just sit at home and watch the television" as well as "You're not important anymore, you're finished!!" (p. 109). Once again, it shows that perhaps the elderly are not the infirmed and helpless individuals that many like to stereotype them as. The respondents themselves said they can tell what the programmers and the larger society think about them according to the programs they put on.

Perhaps the most intriguing point made in this study was that positive imagery is secondary to the elderly who want to see their diversity and experiences truthfully represented in the media. Some felt that elderly characters were only used to "provoke a sympathy vote (frail old person as victim or lonely)" (Healy & Ross, 2002, p. 111). What was most important for the elderly who took part in this study was the feeling that "they often felt marginalized from the TV 'community' because their lives were rendered invisible by the bias towards content aimed at younger age groups" as well as "irritation with the ways in which older people and ageing more generally was portrayed" (p. 112).

This is problematic for many elderly people who, according to the study, tend to think that all old people are lumped together and painted with a brush of homogeneity. This flies in the face of the suggestion, however, from Bradley and Longino that the media portray the elderly as younger as it is "consistent with the notion that older people think of themselves as younger than they are" (2001, p. 21). Some research suggests that elderly media consumers want realistic portrayals while other studies show that they want escapist, image friendly fare. It would seem that a balance needs to be struck between these two ideals as Bradley and Longino espouse, elders "derive their identity not only from past achievements but also from what they would like to accomplish in the future" (p. 21). Others, especially it would seem psychologists, share this notion of the elderly and the effects of reminiscence. Some such as Sherman (1991) write that the elderly internalize aging and use memories of the past to help shape their future in conjunction with new images they may encounter. So, while history clearly plays a role in elderly self-perception and identity, it would seem that new images such as those in the media help to reshape and redefine an elder's look at themselves.

The elderly may deny their age by placing themselves as younger than they chronologically are, but the negative representations still make an impact as they, along with everyone else, internalize these ideals and project them onto other older persons, be it themselves or others in their cohort. Utilizing the constructs of Symbolic Interactionism, this simply serves to perpetuate stereotypes at the same time as an aging individual laments them. This system of reflection and social interaction is tantamount in any notion of identity. While piecing together an interdisciplinary look at aging and identity politics, reflection works in conjunction with ideas of reminiscence as the past, present, and the future all work together to form the multiple self that most individuals are required to employ in this multi-faceted world.

So how can *The Simpsons* be situated within this vast and ever growing look at aging? Well, *The Simpsons* feature many different characters that can be operationalized as elderly. These include Mr Burns, Springfield's oldest and wealthiest resident (at least after the untimely death of Cornelius Chapman from the black widow kiss of Britney Spears), Grampa Simpson, Jasper and the other inhabitants of the Springfield Retirement Castle who are routinely featured, Marge's mother Jackie Bouvier and Homer's mother Mona who are recurring though infrequent characters, the short and wrinkly Hans Moleman, and Mrs. Skinner not to mention the numerous characters who have only appeared a few times at best. The characters all seemingly have one thing in common, they are stereotypes, caricatures of what our culture has deemed to be the standard visualization of aging.

As the voluminous research has demonstrated, these stereotypes are generally negative, feeding off of small truths and exploiting irrational fears. When watching an episode of *The Simpsons,* it would be easy to simply look at the visual representation being presented and ignoring the context or even the audio, deciding that it is an ageist representation. There are many who take this approach. While speaking with a Doctor of Gerontology about *The Simpsons*, he mentioned that while he didn't watch *The Simpsons* with any regularity, he found it to be a negative look at aging. The example that he chose to demonstrate this occurred in the episode "The Mansion Family" (Swartzwelder, 2000, January 23) in which the aging Mr. Burns went to the Mayo Clinic for a check-up after winning the award as Springfield's oldest resident. While getting his physical, the doctor goes to take some blood. He plunges the syringe in Mr. Burns' left arm and it passes all the way through. Amazed, the doctor exclaims "Well, isn't that odd? It's like poking through meringue" to which Burns responds "Try this arm. I saw some blood in there the other day." After his test results come back, Burns meets with his doctor and this exchange takes place:

> **Burns**: Well, doc, I think I did pretty well on my tests. You may shake my hand if you like.
>
> **Doctor**: Well, under the circumstances, I'd rather not.
>
> **Burns**: Eh?
>
> **Doctor**: Mr. Burns, I'm afraid you are the sickest man in the United States. You have everything.

Burns: You mean I have pneumonia?

Doctor: Yes.

Burns: Juvenile diabetes?

Doctor: Yes.

Burns: Hysterical pregnancy?

Doctor: Uh, a little bit, yes. You also have several diseases that have just been discovered -- in you.

Burns: I see. You sure you haven't just made thousands of mistakes?

Doctor: Uh, no, no, I'm afraid not.

Burns: This sounds like bad news.

Doctor: Well, you'd think so, but all of your diseases are in perfect balance. Uh, if you have a moment, I can explain.

Burns: Well ... [*looks at his watch*]

[*the Doctor puts a tiny model house door on his desk*]

Doctor: Here's the door to your body, see? [*bring up some small fuzz balls with goofy faces and limbs from under the desk*] And these are oversized novelty germs. [*points to a different one as he names each disease*] That's influenza, that's bronchitis, [*holds up one*] and this cute little cuddle-bug is pancreatic cancer. Here's what happens when they all try to get through the door at once. [*tries to cram a bunch through the model door. The "germs" get stuck*] [*Stooge-like*] Woo-woo-woo-woo-woo-woo-woo! Move it, chowderhead! [*normal voice*] We call it, "Three Stooges Syndrome."

Burns: So what you're saying is, I'm indestructible!

Doctor: Oh, no, no, in fact, even slight breeze could –

Burns: Indestructible.

While he was arguing that this was a stereotype of the elderly as infirmed and constantly in need of health care, it could also be argued that the irony in this scenes helps to demonstrate the truly ridiculous nature of the images employed. This is a perfect example of how a reading can differ between individuals. This even happens on *The Simpsons* itself in episodes where the family watch TV together.

Examples of this include the family seeing advertisements for products or events that would normally have no interest for them. The power of the media to persuade however is made apparent as the family, or some members of the family, usually Homer, are sucked in and can't imagine living without something that moments before he/they may have been unaware that it even existed. As Douglas Rushkoff (2004) explains,

> "Many episodes are still about what happens on the Simpsons' own television set, allowing the characters to feed off of television, which itself is feeding off of other television. In this self-reflexive circus, it is Bart who is least likely to be fooled by anything. His father, Homer, represents an earlier generation and can easily be manipulated by television commercials and publicity stunts". (p. 297)

After watching a couple of commercials in "Bart The Daredevil" (J. Kogan & W. Wolodarsky, 1990, December 6), both Bart and Homer are convinced that the upcoming Pro Wrestling event should feature "one helluva match" while Lisa refuses to buy into the hype deriding wrestling as choreographed. After the second commercial for a monster truck show, both Bart and Homer are enraptured with the thought of seeing the famed(?) *Truck-O-Saurus*. In this instance, two of the three have bought into what the television was selling, each using a different set of personal information and knowledge to guide their decisions.

Dettmar (2004) uses the example from the episode "And Maggie Makes Three" (J. Chrittenden, 1995, January 22), where the family is watching the program *Knight Boat*, an obvious parody of the David Hasselhoff show *Knight Rider*. As absolutely unbelievable as the plot to the show is, Homer is sucked right in and openly rooting for the boat to help solve crimes. Bart and Lisa, however, are shocked at how outlandish the show is and that certain plot devices reappear every week to aid the boat in its crime solving endeavours. Aided by the constant appearance of "canals, inlets, and fjords", the children of all people deride the show as juvenile. The irony in this particular scene, as Dettmar points out, is thick. While the children mock the program, they still continue to watch, and whether they would like to admit it or not, by using terms like fjord, inlet, and canal, they appear to be learning some important geographical terms that they may have been taught at school, but have seemingly learned from television; the same television that is often referred to as the vast wasteland. It is this irony and subsequent examples that provide the basis for the thesis of this book.

As the examples illustrate, readers bring differing experiences, beliefs and values to the table when decoding a television program and *The Simpsons* is no exception. Just as the family differs in their decoding of television, with Homer often referred to as the passive consumer of television, one who allows the images projected to his screen to entice and lead his decisions, while the children, although often falling into that category, do seem to be able to better distinguish what they see and critically evaluate it. Marge is often portrayed as the most critical of all as she is usually the only character on the show to ever turn the television set off. The idea of encoding and decoding as it applies to the reader/viewer, will be looked at in more detail in the following chapter. As viewer encoding disparity appears on the show, it also appears in real life for media consumers, but what are some of the theoretical underpinnings of postmodernism that lead our evaluation here of *The Simpsons* and its look at aging?

THEORY

Marge: Homey, you know, it's funny. Both my mother and your father seem
pretty lonely.

Homer: Hee hee hee! That is funny.

Marge: Yeah. Anyway, maybe they could go to a matinee together, or
shopping. Or to that room in the library that's always full of
old people? Um...periodicals! That's it.

Homer: Marge, please, old people don't need companionship. They need to
be isolated and studied so it can be determined what nutrients
they have that might be extracted for our personal use.

Marge: Homer, would you please stop reading that Ross Perot pamphlet?
(Oakley & Weinstein, 1994, May 12)

Postmodernism

Postmodernism is a term that means different things to different people and "is a

slippery signifier, producing new meanings and implications practically every time the

word is spoken or cited" (Mittell, 2001, p. 15). Is postmodernism really a theory, or more

of an anti-theory? A paradox exists in that by its definition, it should not be definable.

This is a unique term as well as it has been incorporated into the discourses of many

different and diverse areas such as music, art, architecture, literature, and critical theory.

It is this seemingly constant evolution of the term that often creates confusion among

different theorists. A perfect example of this might be the bifurcation in the writings of

Jameson and Hutcheon, who seem so diametrically opposed, and certainly do disagree on

a lot, but while working within a frame of "postmodernism", approach it from different

perspectives. Jameson writes with a focus on the consumer while Hutcheon writes with the focus on the artist/producer. This of course leads to very different views and approaches to such ideas as aesthetics, pastiche/parody, satire, and irony which are central to the thesis of this book. Before diving directly into these questions, however, it is beneficial to clearly establish the theoretical basis for postmodernism.

It may not even need to be said, but the senses of postmodern theory are so wide and encompassing that truly delineating them or providing a comprehensive genealogy is not possible within the confines of this book. What will be done is to show how and why what we now recognize as postmodern thought began to emerge and its theoretical implications in looking at the representations of aging on *The Simpsons*.

From the writings of Matthew Arnold in the mid 19th century to F.R. Leavis who continued this tradition into the 20th century, the cultural theory of modernism that accompanied this dialogue remained intact. While Arnold was espousing the views that culture preserved the best that had been thought and said, he worked within a strict class-based ideal as he vehemently believed that the Aristocracy was essential and served a larger social purpose. In keeping with his divisive class-based views, Arnold felt that only the elites in society should have access to education and all that trappings that accompanied that as they were the force that moved society, maintained the order, and knew the inner workings whereas the lower classes all served in a laborious capacity to serve the elites. The only other role of the working class was to show obedience to authority and exhibit good manners (Storey, 1998).

F.R. Leavis wrote in the 1930's in support of this cultural theory. What this served to do was promote and reinforce Arnold's ideas of class and their positions in culture and society. Leavis wanted to hearken back to a more distinct era like that of

Arnold, where high culture and legitimate leadership based in an aristocratic model was

not under threat from an emerging mass culture which would serve only to degrade the

masses as it simultaneously stripped control from the elites who had both earned and

deserved their positions. Leavis felt that mass culture was a parasite that would consume

high culture leaving nothing beneficial in its wake.

At the same time, other class based theorists were also operating. The Frankfurt

School emerged and were later followed by the Birmingham School, all offering left

leaning class-based critiques of society. While the Birmingham school studied mass

culture in its own right, the Frankfurt school still criticized the form(s). So while these

four examples may not be operating with the same beliefs or goals, they are all working

with a class-based theory of society and/or culture. These theories, and others like them

are totally within the confines of the postmodern ideal. What is the postmodern ideal?

The "tenets" of postmodernism are essentially based in the repudiation of what is

now considered the modernist era. In *The politics of theory: Ideological positions in the

postmodern debate,* Frederic Jameson (1984a) argues

> ...when we make some initial inventory of the varied cultural artefacts
> that might plausibly be characterized as postmodern, the temptation is
> strong to seek the "family resemblance" of such heterogeneous styles and
> products, not in themselves, but in some common high modernist impulse
> and aesthetic against which they all, in one way or another, stand in
> reaction. (p. 53)

While Jameson recognizes that this is problematic for a number of reasons including the

assumption that this creates both a political and an aesthetic argument to the postmodern debate, he recognizes the importance of history in postmodernism's arguments. So what are these arguments?

Postmodernism sees a breakdown of the distinction between culture and society, at least culture in the Arnoldian sense of the word. This recognizes the emergence of a social order in which the power and importance of the mass media and popular culture become responsible for governing and shaping our social relationships in all of their incarnations. Our reality is now governed by various mass media forms and popular culture begins to dominate our reality. Media have different affects and they can reflect reality, distort reality, and construct reality. This is one of the tenets of postmodern theory.

There is also seen to be an emphasis on style at the expense of substance, what has been referred to as a designer ideology where the narrative of an image becomes subservient to the image itself. This is creating the situation where as participants in this structure, we begin to consume the signs and images around us simply for the sake of consumption as opposed to any use, need, or deeper intrinsic value they may hold or symbolize. At this point, utility and value become unimportant to the aesthetic ideal. It is thus the surface, the outward style of what something looks like that predominates the content, substance, and the meaning of social objects removing any artistic merit or integrity and undermining the narrative function.

This in turn is instrumental in the breakdown of the distinction between art and popular culture. As we increasingly see the signs and imagery of popular culture taking over our defining sense of our lived reality, then our barriers between art and popular culture becomes blurred. In this situation, it harkens to the mass culture critics like those in the Frankfurt school who bemoaned the parasitic nature of mass culture to high culture. The difference here, however, is that most postmodern critics are optimistic about this subversion, and the idea of subversion is critical to this look at representations of aging on *The Simpsons.* As Jameson (1991) and others point out, art is integrated into the economy where it has many different roles, including its role in helping to get people to consume through the use of advertising and other visual media, but also by becoming a distinct commodity unto itself. Postmodern art is unique because it refuses to respect the modernist pretensions and distinctiveness that art once possessed, thus making the breakdown even more prevalent.

Another prominent feature of postmodernism, and one that Jameson (1991) also discusses at length, is the confusion over time and space. This increasing confusion and incoherence in our sense of space and time is happening with such things as mapping redefining how and where we live and with new ideas of time changing the ways in which we organize our lives. Technology has helped to redefine time and space as mass media has created an immediacy to global events and happenings which undermines our previously unified and coherent ideas about space and time, distorting and confusing in the process. With the rapid international flow of money, information, capital, and culture, our linear unities of time and space are disrupted and geographical distance is reconfigured and made incomprehensible in relation to prior ideas.

Perhaps one of the most mentioned tenets of postmodern theory is the idea of the declining importance and power of the all encompassing metanarratives. These include religion, art, science, modernism, and Marxism[9] to name but a few. These metanarratives make absolute, universal, and all embracing claims to knowledge and truth, which postmodern theory rejects with its loss of a continuous linear history and clear sequential events. This scepticism of metanarratives has helped to question their all knowing validity and has thrust them into a decline. Jean-Francois Lyotard contributed to the postmodern canon (which should then paradoxically be rejected?) with his book *The Postmodern Condition: A Report on Knowledge,* penned in 1979. For Lyotard (1984), it was this breakdown in knowledge systems that precipitated the emergence of postmodern thinking. As he wrote about postmodernism, "simplifying to the extreme, I define postmodern as incredulity toward metanarratives" (p. xxiv). It is not directed to any particular knowledge system as postmodernism should reject any claim by theory to absolute knowledge or of any social practice to a universal validity. Applied to the politics of representation, "the postmodern appears to coincide with a general cultural awareness of the existence and power of systems of representations which do not *reflect* society so much as *grant* meaning and value within a particular society" (Hutcheon, 1989, p. 8). So when did these changes start to occur?

John Storey (1998) places postmodernism's beginnings as a sensibility in the works of Susan Sontag and Leslie Fielder that emerged in the late 1950s and the early 1960s. It was an important academic shift that saw a breakdown in the distinction between the modernist cultural ideals of Matthew Arnold and the popular culture of the

---

[9] Of course as mentioned earlier, Frederic Jameson has taken postmodern theory and positioned Marxism within it, rather than theorizing its demise outside of it.

times. Arnold and his latter day adherents like F.R. Leavis preached an elitist mantra that essentially said that the working class should just do their jobs, be respectful to those in positions of authority, and display good manners while the upper class make the decisions as it was their right to do so. There was a clear demarcation in this instance between high and low culture, or as it was increasingly becoming referred to, mass culture. This of course concerned the cultural elites as they saw mass culture as degrading and a threat to their "legitimate" power. Mass culture was viewed as a parasite that would ultimately consume high culture and leave nothing beneficial behind. This seems to fall in line with what Jameson claims commodification has done to high culture, degrading it and creating a blurring of the boundaries between high and popular cultures.

Storey (1998) goes on to explain how modernism's canonization of the "avant-garde revolution" had served to diminish the force and subversion that existed in society by embracing it and assimilating it into a "bourgeois culture" which create a new opponent against which to struggle (p. 170-171). This clearly delineated three distinct time frames and their unique approach to culture. The dominant critical perspective in the cultural writings of Matthew Arnold in the late 19th century simply ignored the folk culture of the time as it praised high cultural pursuits. With the emergence of the modernists, mass culture critics like Leavis and the Frankfurt School not only took notice of the emerging mass culture but fought to protect high culture from its potentially damaging effects. At this stage, high culture such as modern art, jazz, or modern dance was seen as distinct from mass cultural pursuits and was viewed as intellectually engaging, adventurous, and challenging. An emerging postmodern sentiment blurred this distinction as mass or popular culture was studied in its own right. Storey sums up this idea by writing that "Postmodernism was thus born out of a generational refusal of the categorical certainties of high modernism. The insistence of an absolute distinction between high and popular culture came to be regarded as the 'un-hip' assumption of an older generation" (p. 173).

Jonathan Arac writes about the turbulent 1960s and its radicalism and social activism as creating "the urgency of questioning that formed the atmosphere from which postmodernism condensed" (p. ix). This is often considered a key time in the development of postmodern thought. Civil rights, Vietnam, the growing rejection of modernism's elitist attitudes, and a burgeoning feminism are all looked at as precipitates for postmodernism's growing influence on theoretical thought, both in North America and elsewhere in the world. The aesthetics of postmodern texts are integral components of how these postmodern works, whether literary, visual, or otherwise, are able to subvert the fixed ideals of modernism.

Aesthetics

Key to a postmodern aesthetic are some of the main components identified as emblematic of postmodern texts, including television and movies. These are hyper-reflexivity, self-awareness, inter-textuality, and the notion of pastiche and/or parody. These intentionally fly in the face of modern aesthetics, those of a banal realism and generic convention. Rather than existing as nicely labelled boxes to easily compartmentalize postmodern texts, these aesthetic ideals serve in a larger sense to help with the dissolution of generic categorization creating a new field in which an oppositional subversion can operate through the use of these ideals. It is our postmodern sensibilities that allows this mixture of high and the low cultural elements as Jameson and other postmodern theorists believe has occurred within a highly commodified society.

According to Jameson (1984), in the postmodern epoch of late capitalism, we exist in a commodified culture. Everything is a commodity, including art in all its forms, like television. Art is no longer for art's sake, it can only have one purpose and that is to act as a commodity. An entire industry has emerged (the culture industry) that only has one standard; market value. It is in this commodified culture that distinctions between high and low or modern and postmodern begin to disintegrate as they become secondary to the market potential of a commodity which has no inherent value. Believing that in this circumstance, Jameson believes parody is out of a job as he writes:

> In this situation, parody finds itself without a vocation; it has lived, and that strange new thing pastiche slowly comes to take its place. Pastiche is, like parody, the imitation of a peculiar mask, speech in a dead language: but it is a neutral practice of such mimicry, without any of parody's ulterior motives, amputated of the satiric impulse, devoid of laughter and of any conviction that alongside the abnormal tongue you have momentarily borrowed, some healthy linguistic normality still exists. Pastiche is thus blank parody, a statue with blind eyeballs" (p. 65)

To Frederic Jameson, pastiche is a term that essentially implies parody with no bite, lacking the true critical wit and power that existed in the satirical offerings of modernist texts. The term pastiche itself has an interesting history. Ingeborg Hoesterey (1999) shows that the first use of the term pastiche occurred in 1677, in a treatise by the painter Roger de Piles and etymologically relates to the Italian word 'pasticcio' which refers to a hodgepodge of different vegetables. In this contextual situation then, pastiche indicates a painter who has adopted an eclectic style that references many styles and techniques. It later evolved to denote an "ingenious, albeit notorious, copy of a masterwork" (p. 80) and later was adopted into literary criticism. Today it has different meanings for different theorists, and in different contexts. To Jameson then, pastiche is a simple regurgitation of previous ideas and styles in order to sell products and move commodities, it is superficial and holds no larger purpose. There can be no larger purpose under his theoretical musings.

As everything in our society is commodified, according to Jameson, and with the consumer as the focus of artistic production, political content is benign and aesthetic appearances are tantamount to the consumption of images. Hutcheon (1989) agrees with this thesis, but only to a point. Seeing television as primarily reliant on the modernist ideals of realism and transparent representations, it is lacking the qualities required to critique, it can be nothing but a commodity. This change from parody to pastiche occurs when society loses its historical sensibility and is left with a degraded historicism which as Duvall (1999) explains is "an aestheticization of historical periods devoid of the political contradictions that those styles embodied" (p.375). As such, this pastiche of imagery serves to demean, belittle, cannibalize and subsequently erase or displace history by reconfiguring it outside of its original situation; its original voice. Thus it is the surface, the aesthetic that matters in postmodern texts. Subscribing to the theory allows no room for any relevant social critique or opposition. This is where the bridge has to be made to Linda Hutcheon's postmodernism, where the 'critique' is postmodernism and ultimately results from the aesthetic devices employed.

As mentioned earlier, Hutcheon's approach to postmodernism has a different focus than Jameson's, looking more at the role and contribution of the artist or producer than at the consumer as in Jameson's model. Hutcheon thus has a differing view on what constitutes postmodernism than do others, namely Jameson. To her, postmodernism is meant to operate this way, in a contradictory manner which may be partly responsible for its political power as she sees it. It is contradiction, with both the modern and postmodern, that highlights and undermines. This juxtaposition of ideas creates a self-reflexive history that is crucial in utilizing postmodernism as a political tool through aesthetic devices.

Hutcheon (1989) does agree with other theorists that the manifestations for postmodernism are broad and diverse as she identifies "architecture, literature, photography, film, painting, video, dance, music, and elsewhere" (p. 1) as areas in our cultural world where postmodernism and its aesthetic ideals are evident. Since postmodernism began, and continues to function as a check against the absolute claims of metanarratives, postmodern texts then

> de-naturalize some of the features of our way of life; to point out that those entities that we unthinkingly experience a 'natural', (they might even include capitalism, patriarchy, liberal humanism) are in fact 'cultural'; made by us, not given to us. (p. 2)

So unlike Jameson, Hutcheon sees postmodernism as subversive, and primarily due to one important quality, the use of irony.

Irony

Wayne Booth (1974) sees irony as moving "from the known to the unknown" or as "saying one thing and meaning the opposite" (p.34). In his estimation, this leaves the reader the task of having to reconstruct the sense of the ironic text which of course requires competence on the part of the decoder, or in the case of *The Simpsons,* the viewer. Booth also explains how, as a result of this requisite competence, irony can succeed or ultimately fail and that is the risk that the author or producer must take. As a result, irony "risks disaster more aggressively than any other device. But if it succeeds, it will succeed more strongly than any literal statement can do" (p. 41-42). As Dettmar (2004) suggests in his article, *The Simpsons* succeeds for many reasons, not the least of which is that it encourages a critical evaluation of our world. Booth (1974) further explains that the readers feel as though their contributions to the text as a reader are crucial in its reconstruction where as he sees the reader as actually subjugated to the will of the author. This appears contradicted later, however, when he writes that it is totally possible for two readers to decode the exact same text in opposing manners. Where then is the will of the author imposed? And why only on one of the readers? Hall (1980), offers the idea of oppositional readings which Booth seemingly ignores, or fails to recognize.

Rejecting the traditional mass communication model based on the idea of sender-receiver, Hall (1980) suggests that this model is incorrect as reception isn't that transparent, that cut and dry, but involves embedded messages and ideologies that help to shape our perceptions of the real, of our reality. This is where the politicization of the media begins as we move from a message and effects discourse and recognize the role of the viewer as a competent (or not) decoder of messages, granted agency through our critical reflection on the text. It is in the "discursive domain" that we see social life mapped out, where we accept or contest this, and where meanings are organized into what Hall sees as a hierarchy.

In his paper Hall (1980) identifies "three hypothetical positions from which decodings of a televisual discourse may be constructed" (p. 130). The first of the positions is referred to as the *dominant hegemonic position*. The theory behind this position implies that the reader/viewer/decoder is receiving messages as a reflection of society. This then is essentially the transparency that Hall talks about where agency or reflexivity is stalled, effectively resulting in an inactive audience. In this code, the message is deciphered entirely as it was encoded and intended to be read while working within the hegemony of the dominant code, of which a professional code is at work as well. Hall explains that this "serves to reproduce the dominant definitions precisely by bracketing their hegemonic quality and operating instead with displaced professional codings" (p. 131) which in turn serve to present the message as researched, objective, common sense, neutral, and professionally presented. There is often, however, disagreements between the dominant and the professional codes and they can be looked at separate to each other though one works within the other.

Hall (1980) looks next at what he terms the *negotiated code* and sees it as the most commonly used code in the integration of media messages where the majority of the audience mostly seem to understand that the messages they are seeing have been "dominantly defined and professionally signified" (p. 131). So while there is an element of agency present in this model, the actual reading of the code is highly dependent on the experiences and knowledge base and seems to contain an element of ambivalence, at least in the respect that individuals see issues in the larger scheme of things and meanings are perceived in the "national interest". This is not always the case as often inconsistencies and exceptions appear based on an individuals situation. Hall explains how the dominant idea of low wages to combat inflation is in the national interest and many believe this idea to be a taken for granted approach to economics, that same person, however, may not want to actually accept lower pay in their job. These disjunctures are often seen by the encoders as a miscommunication or failure to properly communicate.

Lastly, Hall (1980) identifies the decoder who reads the media messages as ideological imposition as operating within the *oppositional code*. In this mode, the viewer understands "both the literal and the connotative inflection given by a discourse but…decode the message in a globally contrary way" (p. 132). In other words the audience working within the oppositional code decodes the preferred code of meaning but then reconstructs it in another framework, in an oppositional manner to that intended. This places agency with the viewer and allows for the reconstruction of ironic texts, including television, and politicizes the decoding of signified meanings, the politicization that Hutcheon sees as inherent in ironic parody.

As Ryan (1992) notes, "irony can be an illusive element—hard to pin down, not easily defined" (p. 59). Thus, decoding of ironic texts can be problematic for various reasons. One of these is the notion that irony is currently "used primarily to reinforce and reinscribe an 'in-group' (wink-wink, nudge-nudge)" (Dettmar, 2004, p. 85). This position posits irony counter to the views of most theorists, including Hutcheon. It says that rather than being overtly political or truly critiquing texts, it serves only as an affirmation to the hip and cool of their hipness and coolness. Dettmar points to Jedediah Purdy as a prominent proponent of this viewpoint. Purdy writes that

> We practice a form of irony insistently doubtful of the qualities that would make us take another person seriously: the integrity of personality, sincere motivation, the idea that opinions are more than symptoms of fear and desire. We are wary of hope, because we see little that can support it. Believing in nothing much, especially not in people, is a point of vague

pride, and conviction can seem embarrassingly naïve. (as quoted in
Dettmar, p. 85)

This of course hearkens to a notion of irony that coincides with a modernist ideal of irony

and its elitist beliefs. By definition then, postmodernism and postmodern irony are

subversive of this ideal because, as Dettmar explains, it is "more democratic, more

inclusive, more open and fluid" (p. 86). It is this element of subversion that gives

postmodern irony its strength in creating oppositional meaning.

Irony though, is not the sole property of the author or producer as readers/viewers

have an equal share in its operation. This is made readily apparent as well in *The Simpsons*

as was mentioned earlier. In episodes where the family is watching television together,

what they see and the message it sends is often perceived differently by the various

members of the family. It is the use of irony in *The Simpsons* which allows for the

possibility of subversion.

To Linda Hutcheon (1989), irony is the ingredient that transforms the aesthetics of

postmodernism from Jameson's pastiche of images or "blank parody", and into a parodic

textual entity that points out and questions the conventional and through the decoding

abilities of the reader (or viewer), incorporates the sense of agency missing from Jameson's

aesthetic model, allowing for the politicization and historicization of the text. As she

explains, one of the overarching tenets of postmodernism is its historicizing and

politicizing of texts, making them available for critiquing. Postmodernism

> takes the form "self-conscious, self-contradictory, self-undermining
> statement. It is rather like saying something whilst at the same time putting
> inverted commas around what is being said. The effect is to highlight, or
> 'highlight', and to subvert, or 'subvert', and the mode is therefore a
> 'knowing' and an ironic—or even 'ironic'—one. (p.1)

It is this subversion of the "natural" that Hutcheon feels are called into question, pointing out that they are not in fact natural, but culturally constructed. It is this realization that gives postmodern irony its strength. Quoting postmodern theorist Victor Burgin (1986), the 'politics of representation' recognizes the ideological grounding in all forms of representation and it is the "the self-reflexive, parodic art of the postmodern" that serves to underline this with its ironic qualities (p. 55). This is the intrinsic political component of postmodernism.

It is here that Hutcheon takes Roland Barthes notion of "doxa" as public opinion or 'The Voice of Nature' (p. 3) and thus suggest that the postmodern elements serve to 'de-doxify' or denaturalize the inherent politics of our cultural representation. It is the aesthetics of postmodern texts that demonstrate the political dimension of our representations and ultimately serves to critique them. This then allows us to recognize that everything we experience is "cultural", in other words, "mediated by representations" (p. 34). According to Hutcheon's definition, postmodernism is the means by which we question our reality, our representations and our meanings; this includes representations of the elderly. It is here that we can look closer at parody and how it operates within this postmodern schema.

Parody

Parody, according to Hutcheon (1985, 1989) is central to theories of postmodern aestheticism as it borrows from the past to show how the representations of our present have evolved, where they began, and what the ideological implications of this are. Borrowing from the past, parody uses irony as a "value-problematizing, de-naturalizing form of acknowledging the history…of representations" (1989, p. 94) as well as the

political implications of these representations. Answering her critics, Hutcheon addresses

their concerns that parody is nothing more than a powerless pastiche of imagery that

doesn't consider the original context and history thus falling short of any political

ambitions. This is countered by Hutcheon as she sees that

> postmodern parody does not disregard the context of the past
> representations it cites, but uses irony to acknowledge the fact that that we
> are inevitably separated from that past today—by time and by the
> subsequent history of those representations. (p. 94)

So postmodern representation *can't* ignore the context and the history of past

representations, by acknowledging the past, it can't help but showcase the passage

of time and maintain the continuum that some theorists believe is missing in

parody.

Hutcheon (1985) speaks of parody as being more than a simple inter-textual

reference. There is the implication in parody of "intention to parody another work

(or set of conventions) and both a recognition of that intent and an ability to find

and interpret the backgrounded text in its relation to parody" (p. 22). When The

Simpsons parody other texts like movies, books, TV shows, or even paintings, they

do so in a matter that recognizes the history, showcases the passage of time adding

a political characteristic, and utilize irony in an attempt to create an arena for

criticism.

It is irony that takes representations and highlights the contradictions, the

processes of production, and calls attention to them asking for a critique. As with

ironic readings, parodic readings (which of course can and do often include ironic elements) require the participation of the audience. As Hutcheon (1985) believes, as parody offers us a look at the representations of the past by "giving it a new and often ironic context, it makes similar demands upon the reader, but these are demands more on his or her knowledge and recollection than on his or her openness to play" (p. 5). Thus it is the readers knowledge base that dictates which parodic and ironic devices are able to potentially subvert the history of the representations. This is how *The Simpsons* utilizes ironic parody. Of course it is possible to miss the parody and the ironic elements contained within, but fortunately *The Simpsons* offer clues and alert us to potential parodic, ironic, and satiric elements.

The titles of Simpsons' episodes are a perfect indication to viewers that parody is a force at work on the show. Many of the titles directly parody or indirectly allude to other texts, be they film, television, book, or music for instance. With episode titles like "Cape Feare", "The Telltale Head", "You Only Move Twice", and "Behind the Laughter" serving as direct parodies of famous texts. The importance with these particular episodes is that they don't only parody the title, the episode itself is also a parody of the original. In "Cape Feare", Sideshow Bob is paroled from prison and has revenge on his mind, revenge on young Bart Simpson for sending him to prison after foiling his plans to frame Krusty the Klown. The original text here is the movie(s) "Cape Fear" with identical storylines and referents. "The Telltale Head" parodies both the title and the theme of the famed Edgar Allen Poe story as Bart removes the head from the town founder's statue only to feel guilt and hear it talk to him. In "You Only Move Twice", Homer gets a great job offer and moves the family only to find out the his new boss, Mr. Scorpio, is bent on world domination and the underlying story of the episode parodies a James Bond movie. "You Only Live Twice" is the title of a popular Bond film. The "Behind the Laughter" episode is a direct parody of the "Behind the Music" on the VH1 music channel. A clearly postmodern episode it breaks the barrier of reality on the show[10] by treating the members of the family as actors playing characters. These are a synopsis and an ad from the TV Guide on the week this episode originally aired.

> [*TV Guide Close-Up*] In the sharp 11th-season finale, the Simpsons are studied in a Behind the Music-style documentary depicting their rise to stardom -- and the "private hell" that followed. VH1's Jim Forbes narrates their story, beginning with the evolution of The Simpsons TV show, from Homer's original idea called "My Funny Family." The series took off, but the physical comedy took a toll on Homer, bringing an addiction to painkillers. Wild spending, bad investments and tax problems ensued, leading to an incident at the Iowa State Fair that split them up, and prompted solo projects -- until Willie Nelson stepped in.

> [*TV Guide ad*] When the Camera Stops ... Who Are the Real Simpsons? Tonight, see a side of them you've never seen before! Bart: Eat My Shorts? I'd never say that! Homer: Be quiet! And take your anti-growth hormones. (Rose, 2003)

It is instances like these, in addition to numerous others, that can help to alert the viewers of the parodic elements at work.

---

[10] Of course as an animated program, there can be no "reality", but for the sake of the argument, *The Simspons* is treated as a televisual reality, that is to say as a family represented by a father, mother, and three children on a television program week to week in a programmed sense of the real. It's not real, and we as viewers know that but in order to enjoy all the layers at work, we must treat it as "real". This episode ignores the history of the show and treats it as it really is, a cast of characters as opposed to a real family. A shattering of the illusion of reality in an entirely unreal situation. Akin to the idea of kayfabe in Professional Wrestling.

One argument made against parody is that it is simply an imitation and not a critical analysis of the original text or the representations contained within. This of course would be characterized by Jameson as pastiche, a toothless parody. Hutcheon (1985) agrees that parody can be loosely situated as imitation but is characterized by its ironic inversion and is inherently so much more than a simple replication. Since parody can have many different intents, "from the ironic and playful to the scornful and ridiculing", while being an imitation in the strictest sense, it is "characterized by ironic inversion" and is thus "repetition with critical distance, which marks differences rather than similarities" (p. 6). The differences parodied don't always have to be other specific texts either as they can be conventions or genres as well.

In the episode "The Old Man and the C Student" (Thacker, 1999) for example, a direct reference is made to a specific text as a scene is parodied from "One Flew Over the Cuckoo's Nest". In the episode, the residents of the "Springfield Retirement Castle" have been treated as virtual prisoners in their home, unable to leave and at the whimsy of the staff, much like the mental patients in "One Flew Over the Cuckoo's Nest". There is a scene where a young Bart Simpson has been forced to volunteer in the home and while horrified at first, he soon realises that their existence isn't very fulfilling. As the residents enjoy a game called "Imagination" where they wear life vests and pretend to sail, the opportunity arises for Bart to help them escape and enjoy real boating and he rallies the group.

Bart: Okay, she's gone. Let's break out of here and have some fun.

[*The old people murmur amongst themselves*]

Abe: If I get up, somebody'll take my chair.

Jasper: You got that right. It's the only one left with
padding [*the old people touch the padding and say,
"padding," in a monotone voice*]

Bart: [*to an old Native American man*] What about you,
chief? Don't you wanna be free like the eagle?

Chief: Oh, I don't live here. I'm dropping off Indian
Casino Pamphlets. Vote yes on prop 217.
[*The chief leaves by breaking the window with a water
fountain, and jumping through the broken glass.
Crazy Old Man comes over*]

Crazy Old Man: You know, the door was open, Chief Break-everything!

Bart:Come on people, you don't want to stay in a place
where they vacuum you while you sleep.

Jasper: They do what now?

Bart:Now's our chance. Let's go! [*the old people agree
and follow Bart. Lisa comes back*]

Lisa: Oh no, Bart has stolen the elderly!
[*the chief breaks the window with another water
fountain, and jumps back in*]

Chief: Forgot my hat. [*gives Lisa a pamphlet, then runs
away*]

"Chief", as Bart refers to him, looks almost exactly like the character Chief

Bromden in the classic film "One Flew Over the Cuckoos Nest". In the film,

Chief is forced to leave the asylum and does so by pulling a sink station from the

floor and tossing it through a window, the window through which he escapes. On

The Simpsons, Chief did not need to break the window with the water fountain as he was reminded, "the door was open". And he surely didn't need to break another window to get his hat back. A direct parody with an ironic and ridiculing bite. As mentioned, there is also generic parody.

In the episode "A Star Is Burns" (Keeler, 1995, March 5), Springfield holds a film festival. Local resident Barney Gumble directs and stars in a movie that shows during the festival. It is in black and white, is stark and emotional with a tormented and introspective veneer. It features the film noir conventions utilized by directors such as Orson Welles or even the haunting emptiness of a Bergman film. In the episode "Bart the Murderer" (Swartzwelder, 1991, October 10), while parodic links can be made to specific films including "Goodfellas", "The Godfather", or "Raging Bull", it is the overall generic parody of the classic gangster film that is at work here. Character voice-overs, missing persons, a "family" outside of the regular family unit comprised of fellow gangsters, and stereotypes of ethnic and gender roles abound in this generic parody. As such, not all parodic references need to be to a specific text although they can also address both the individual text and generic conventions.

These strategies of parody, irony, and satire are employed in *The Simpsons* as a social critique, and work as such. They help to alert the viewer to the history, and historical relations between aging and the cultural representations which we see everyday. By showing the viewer parodies of these stereotypes and generally unflattering representations in an often ironic or satiric way, it serves as a deconstruction. When we see elderly characters instantly falling asleep at any given second for no reason other than they are elderly and cannot control themselves, we realise that this is ironically parodying the idea in our society that elderly people tend to sleep more than middle aged or younger individuals. By using the instantaneous irony of this cultural representation we are encouraged to ask ourselves "where does this idea come from?" or "why do we think this about older people?". By framing a representation of the elderly in such a light, we are directed to question it, rethink it, and even to dispute it. This is, of course, postmodernism at work. It is employed with regularity and with success on *The Simpsons*.

CASE STUDY

*The family drop Grampa off at the retirement home after another miserable third Sunday of the month' outing with Grampa. The sign out front reads "**Springfield Retirement Castle -Where the elderly can hide from the inevitable**"*

Homer: Dad, next time we see you we'll do something more fun.

Abe: Ohhhhhhh. What could be more fun than today's trip to the liquor store. [Angrily] Thanks for the beef Jerky!

Marge: Say goodbye to Grampa everyone.

Bart & Lisa: BYE! *[Homer speeds away]*

Bart: Ya know, Grampa kinda smells like that trunk in the garage where the bottoms all wet.

Lisa: Nuh-uh. He smells more like a photo lab.

Homer: Stop it! Both of you. Grampa smells like a regular old man which is more like a hallway in a hospital.

Marge: Homer, that's terrible. We should be teaching the children to treasure the elderly.

(Kogen & Wolodarsky, 1991, March 28)

In order to understand the theoretical implications of postmodern theory and how it is applied to *The Simpsons,* one complete episode, as well as instances from other individual shows, will be looked at to demonstrate how the theoretical underpinnings are responsible for creating a positive representation of age. Using instances of irony, parody, and satire, it will be established how, according to Linda Hutcheon's theoretical model, these serve to create a subversion of the stereotypes they seem to employ. The episode being analyzed here is "Old Money" (Kogen & Wolodarsky, 1991, March 28). This particular episode has been selected for examination as it has its focus on characters that are elderly and there are many overt references to aging and stereotypes or ideals associated with age. As this episode and the further examples utilized traverse a large section of the series, it shows how *The Simpsons* has maintained a stable style in its writing and use of representations. This enables this episode to clearly show how postmodern theories of aesthetics, irony, parody, and satire can be applied to *The Simpsons*. References will be culled from other episodes that demonstrate this ideal as well, but as the episodes may not directly deal with aging as this one does, they will not be examined in their entirety. Parody is used on *The Simpsons* with regularity as each episode features multiple examples, and this episode is no different.

First, in order to recognize *The Simpsons* as a postmodern text, which is integral to Hutcheon's model, it is important to see how the aesthetics of the program can be classified as postmodern. As mentioned earlier, some of the indicative postmodern aesthetic devices include intertextuality, self-reflexivity, hyper-awareness, and the utilization of parody. *The Simpsons* are rife with examples of these strategies. In the episode "Bart vs. Thanksgiving" (Meyer, 1990, November 22) from the second season, Bart and Homer are seated on the couch watching the Macy's Thanksgiving Day Parade on the television. As the announcers voice-overs introduce the large balloon floats belonging to cartoon characters, Bart has no idea who these characters are. First one introduced is Rocky and Bullwinkle. Homer chuckles because Bullwinkle's antler has sprung a leak. Bart looks oddly at the TV and asks his father

> **Bart**: Who the hell is that?
>
> **Homer**: Bullwinkle

Bart: Who? Wait a minute. Who's that?

Homer: Underdog. Don't you know anything?

Bart: Well I know it wouldn't hurt them to use some cartoons made in the last 50 years.

Homer: Son, this is a tradition. If you start building a balloon for every flash in the pan cartoon character, you'll turn the parade into a farce.

As Homer imparts this last piece of wisdom, the shot of the "scene" changes from in front of the couch looking directly at the front of the characters, to a shot from behind, looking over their shoulders so that between the heads we can watch the parade on the television. As they are turned to each other and talking, and as Homer explains that flash in the pan characters will turn the Macy's parade into a farce, we see a Bart Simpson balloon, tethered to a float, pass by on the TV screen. A perfect, and early, example of how *The Simpsons* uses hyper-reflexivity in its makeup. This scene is important for numerous reasons. It introduces the elements of self-awareness and inter-textuality and helps to destroy the illusion of fiction and reality that is emblematic of modernist texts. There is also an element of irony here as well since *The Simpsons*, far from being a flash in the pan, is now the longest running comedy program on prime time American television. While this may not have been ironic per se at the time this episode was produced, it has become ironic after the fact, and as *The Simpsons* are available in syndication, in many markets 5 or more times a day, it now carries a strong irony in its rebroadcast. This is, of course, not the only example of these aesthetic devices.

In the introduction to a few episodes as we see the family arrive home from their respective days, they run into the living room headed for the couch only to miss the mark, fly off the edge of the screen past the film's sprockets and into empty space. In an episode of *The Simpsons* from the 15th season entitled "Milhouse Doesn't Live Here Anymore" (Chambers & Chambers, 2004, February 15), the program once again references itself. While on a field trip to the Museum of Television (which offers free Emmys to the first 1000 visitors), Bart and his friend Milhouse are walking through the corridors of the museum while they discuss the fact that Milhouse will be leaving Springfield with his mother. As they walk along, oblivious to the artefacts and displays, they pass through the "Hall of Nosy Neighbors". The first statue display is for Mrs. Kravitz, Samantha and Darren's neighbour who was continually spying on them in the 1960s sitcom *Bewitched*. The second display was for Mr. Roper, the landlord and busybody from *Three's Company*. The third and final display in this hallway featured Ned Flanders, the Simpsons' neighbour. The hyper-reflexivity and self-awareness here is evident, but it also carries an irony in that Flanders, while he pops up in the show a lot, is not really an intentionally nosy neighbour, at least not in the same sense as Mrs. Kravitz and Mr. Roper. In fact, Homer probably noses in on Flander's business more so than the other way around. Of course, Milhouse and Bart are embroiled in a discussion of Milhouse's impending move to Capitol City, and so do not see the Flanders statue. It is references like these in which the writers of *The Simpsons*, rather than eschewing a rich cultural tradition in television genres, embrace it with ironic parody. But what about more direct references to aging?

"Old Money"

In "Old Money", parodic references are made to many other texts, including the 1936 film *Mr. Deeds Goes to Town* starring Gary Cooper, the 1932 film *If I Had a Million*, also starring Gary Cooper, and the 1963 film *Tom Jones* as well as alluding to scenes from *A Christmas Carol* and Neil Diamond's *Jazz Singer*. The episode begins with the scene at the start of this chapter; the family drops Grampa off after their monthly visit. After returning Grampa to the Springfield Retirement Castle, the family speeds off when the discussion turns to what does Grampa smell like? Bart feels that Grampa smells "like that trunk in the garage where the bottoms all wet". Lisa believes Grampa smells more like "a photo lab". Homer chastises his children with a loud and abrupt "Stop it. Both of you". As we prepare for Homer to remind the kids to respect their elders, or that Grampa is his father and their blood and as such their comments are mean and hurtful, his admonishment is that Grampa "smells like a regular old man which is more like a hallway in a hospital". So rather than stopping the children, or explaining that the elderly are to be respected, he simply corrects their stereotypes with another, that old people are antiseptic and smell like hospitals. This is of course where Marge assumes her role as the "responsible" parent.

She chides her husband reminding him that as parents they should be "teaching the children to treasure the elderly. You know, we'll be old someday". And there is the ultimate irony, of course lost on Homer until now. Instantly fearful that what he has done to his father may happen to him, Homer gasps and asks "You kids won't put me in a home like I did to my dad will ya?" Bart of course has to think this over as it may have appeal. Like father like son. This of course greatly worries Homer, fearful that his actions may come full circle later in life. Marge suggests that they need to set a positive example with Grampa and Homer readily agrees. He is not doing this out of any altruistic feelings for his father, he simply hopes to avert being placed in a retirement home by his children. Hoping to create a more positive family excursion, the decision is made that next time, they will all go to "Discount Lion Safari".

We next see Abe as he enter his room, angrily mumbling about his day with the family. He pulls open the top drawer in his dresser, slams the beef jerky into it and closes the drawer. This isn't the first time his family day consisted of a trip to the liquor store; his drawer is overflowing with beef jerky. The residents are lined up like cattle at the dispensary window to receive their daily medication. Abe is given the wrong cup of pills and through this mix up, he meets Beatrice Simmons. While he tries to explain the error to the nurse by pointing out that he should have "two red ones for my back spasms, a yellow one for my arrhythmia, and two of…" he looks to his right and notices Bea, "the bluest eyes I've ever seen in my life". After they have the situation righted, and notice an initial attraction between them, they sit down and begin a seductive pill taking campaign, alluding to the famous dining scene in the movie *Tom Jones,* but with less seduction and more medication. After much awkwardness and lamenting that "you'd think this would get easier with time" and mentioning how they are acting "like a couple of stupid punk teenagers", a date is made.

Looking around at the background as Grampa walks down the hallway to Bea's room, and also in the other scenes from the retirement home, you can't help but notice that plaster is cracked, ceilings are crumbling, wallpaper is peeling off and there is a general feeling of deterioration in the building. All the characters, however, never take notice as it is just the way that things are. Picking up Bea, they go dancing, sing to each other, and while the same song plays, we are shown scenes of subsequent dates where they feed pigeons in the park, share a milkshake at the malt shop, and stroll along the beach. The scenes help to create different feelings about the couple, and about the aged.

The first scene shows them dancing and laughing and makes no overt references to their age as they float across the dance floor, nimbly and effortlessly. The scene in the malt shop hearkens back to the stereotypical date in the 50s, at least as it has been presented in movies, TV, and even comic books. This lends a period feeling to the piece, establishing a specific era for the characters and demonstrating the ideal put forward by Bultena & Powers (1979) with their "denial of aging" theory. The characters in this situation, rather than falling into the stereotypical roles that the elderly are seen in, deny their age by reverting to something from their youth, namely a date at a malt shop. This can also be applied to their walk on the beach, often the mantra for young people attempting to attract a member of the opposite sex through a singles ad. This creates a juxtaposition with their other activity, sitting on a bench feeding birds. Countless movies have used the stereotype to show lonely elderly people, sitting on a bench and feeding the birds. But they are not alone, they are together and they are happy. Does this subvert the stereotype? Does it at least cause us to question the history of these representations? And even though they are strolling hand-in-hand down the beach, in this scene they wear Hawaiian print shirts and Abe is wearing shorts looking like the prototypical representation of an elderly tourist. They both have a lot of skin showing and it is wrinkly. Perhaps excessively so. As well, as they stroll along, they are passed by a large turtle. An irony in this situation is that, while it demonstrates how slow they are (perhaps because of their age, and the notion of old and slow comes up again later in this episode), turtles live a long time, longer than most other animals. Apparently old turtles are still quicker than old humans. The scene ends with them back at the home. Abe is playing the piano, both are singing, the floor is lifting and the walls are peeling. We then jump to a new day.

It is Bea's birthday and Abe needs to buy a special gift for his girlfriend, unfortunately, the only store he knows is the military surplus store, so he goes in looking for a gift. Unable to find a suitable gift, he is shown the store across the street which may be more appropriate, "Grandma's World". The signs over the aisles follow stereotypes of items that are associated with old ladies such as "hard candies", "doilies", "picture frames", "sea shell soap", "sachets", and "potpourri". Abe decides on a wool shawl. The clerk has to check the "active wear" department to get a price check. The idea of a wool shawl conjures images of an old lady in a rocking chair knitting a blanket. Is that what we see as "active" for seniors?

While Abe is preparing for his date with Bea by wrapping her gift, Homer barges into the room reminding his father that it is the third Sunday of the month again, the one day it would seem when the Simpson family feels obligated to spend time with the aging Simpson. Grampa, is wrapping the present and not so politely tells his son that he "can't go, it's my girlfriend Bea's birthday" to which Homer mockingly replies "Ohhhh, you have a girlfriend hee hee hee, well, happy birthday Bea" as he talks to an empty chair. Homer's assumption in this instance is that his father is senile and has an imaginary girlfriend, and despite Grampa's protestations to the contrary, he is hauled away and forced to participate in the outing. While they drive along in the car, Grampa tries to open the door and escape only to curse the childproof doors. This should be ironic as Grampa is the oldest, and the patriarch of the Simpson family, he is treated as a child, but many elderly are so the irony is seemingly lost. While at the "Discount Lion Safari", the family gets lost, stuck, are surrounded by lions, and are forced to spend the night in the park meaning Grampa will get home too late for his date. As one of the park security members arrive on the scene in the early morning, he fires his shotgun and watches the lions scramble. This alerts the family and after rolling down his window, Homer is greeted with "Mr. Simpson I presume". This alludes to the reporter who travelled to Africa to find famous explorer David Livingstone and upon finally meeting him in the jungle uttered the now famous, "Dr. Livingstone I presume". Another example of how *The Simpsons* utilize parodic references as an inter-textual device.

As Grampa returns from this disastrous family outing, he runs into the Springfield Retirement Castle exclaiming

> **Abe**: Outta my way, I've got a date with an angel.
>
> **Jasper**: You don't know how right you are Abe.
>
> **Abe**: What?
>
> **Jasper**: Ummm, sorry to be the one to tell you this but, uh, Bea passed away last night.
>
> **Abe**: Ohhhhhhhhh no.
>
> **Jasper**: It was her ticker. Doc said her left ventricle burst.

> **Abe**: Oh no Jasper. They may say she died of a burst ventricle, but I
> know she died of a broken heart.

The viewer here, at least the viewer who took grade nine human biology, knows that a "burst ventricle" is for all intents and purposes, a broken heart. We fade to black, which is important as *The Simpsons* rarely use fade to black as a transitional device, perhaps reflecting here the death of a character. We next see family and friends at the grave site for the funeral.

The rain is falling as six elderly men struggle to pull the casket out of the hearse and carry it to the grave.

> **Abe**: I can tell she really cared for me, she didn't make me a pall bearer.
>
> **Homer**: I can't tell you how sorry I am dad.
>
> **Abe**: Is someone talking to me? I didn't hear anything.
>
> **Homer**: OH NO! Dad's lost his hearing.
>
> **Abe**: No you idiot, I'm ignoring you. You made me miss the last
> precious moments of Bea's life. I'll never speak to you again. I
> haavvvve nooo soooonnn. (*rips jacket*).
>
> *Homer cries.*

The admonishment that "I have no son" is a direct allusion to "The Jazz Singer" starring Neil Diamond[11]. In this movie the main character (played by Diamond) defies his strict Jewish father and pursues his dream of being a popular singer. This movie is parodied in even more detail in the episode "Like Father, Like Son" where we as viewers learn that

---

[11] The original "Jazz Singer" starred Al Jolson and was released in 1927. Considered one of the movies ultimately responsible for the demise of the silent pictures, it was mostly musical numbers with a limited number of conversational sequences. The parody in *The Simpsons* and this line in particular, is thus to the Neil Diamond version.

Krusty the Klown is really named Herschel Krustofsky and has defied his rabbi father by becoming an entertainer. Krusty and his father are estranged and the Simpsons set out to get them back together and which time Rabbi Krustofsky also uses the "I have no son" line. Parodic references are not restricted to film or television texts either.

In "Old Money", as Grampa walks the streets of Springfield thinking about whom to give his money to, he looks around to see the homeless, the dilapidated "Pub ic Lib ary", and the other needy groups and individuals. Needing time to think, he stops in a diner for a cup of coffee and in a "shot" reminiscent of the famous Edward Hopper painting "Nighthawks", Grampa is sidled up to the diner counter as we see in from outside. This parody of the original painting serves a few purposes. First, it reminds the viewer of the original, and the feeling of emptiness or loneliness that it invokes. The figures in the diner of the original, looking contemplative and seemingly lost in their own thoughts give us a window into what Grampa is presumably feeling at this time, and we can see this in how he is depicted in this still shot. It also serves the purpose that Hutcheon mentions, in that it helps to establish the context and the history of the original. As the painting was created and placed in the 1940's, it hearkens back to a different time, ironically a time when a younger Grampa may have been seated, drinking coffee and thinking about the war. Obviously Grampa is older, and that removal from the time of the original text juxtaposed against the now, shows and highlights the history of both texts, rather than ignoring or ahistoricizing as Jameson might claim. This is what Hutcheon (1985) refers to as "trans-contextualization" (p. 8) as an original work, Hopper's painting "Nighthawks", has been incorporated into another medium, television animation, and works within the original context to create an ironic difference. *The Simpsons* regularly reference other texts in each episode, often as many as 10 or 15 overt references can be found as these parodic and intertextual references help to place the program on a larger continuum of cultural programming from early TV, film, music, and animation which, despite what Jameson claims, helps to give a historical referent to both *The Simpsons* and the texts that they parody.

We find out from Bea's attorney that Abe has inherited $106,000 from his girlfriend. Unsure of what exactly to do with the sudden windfall, Grampa decides to give the money to "truly needy causes". In the movie "Mr. Deeds Goes to Town", the main character Longfellow Deeds also inherited a large sum of money and decided to give it to needy causes. In both, characters are lined up and one at a time make a proposal to their potential benefactors for funding. In the movie "If I Had a Million", an aging millionaire is upset with those around him, family and otherwise, so before he dies he picks eight people at random from the city directory to whom he will give his money. One of the lucky eight is a resident of a decaying retirement home who uses the windfall to restore the building as well as gain control in order to implement softer rules. In "Old Money", Abe Simpson ultimately uses his money to do the same thing.

However, shortly after being informed of his windfall, the director of the "Springfield Retirement Castle" comes in to schmooze with Grampa Simpson.

> **Director**: (*opening door to Grampa's room*) Mr. Simpson?
>
> **Abe**: AHHHHHH! What is it?
>
> **Director**: I couldn't help overhearing about your new found fortune and uh, let me assure you that here at the Springfield Retirement Castle, money does make a difference.

Abe: Ehhhhh?

Director: I mean, there are rub downs, and then there are rub downs.

Abe: Listen you bloodsucker. Has it ever occurred to you that old folks deserve to be treated like human beings whether they have money or not?

Director: Yes, but it passes.

Abe: (*mumbling as he exits his room*) ...son of a...

In a situation like this, humour is used to present what can be perceived as a real issue in elder care with residents and retirement home owners or directors. When Grampa lashes back at the director, he presents an argument that is on the minds of many elderly. This also parodies "If I had a Million" as the retirement home resident that was randomly picked to get money was having issues with her home director and by putting the money into the home, ultimately was able to subvert their authority and have their position changed, to the benefit of all the residents. In this situation Grampa will use the money to fix up the old folks' home and the funds will then be available to treat old folks like human beings, whether they have money or not. The postmodern aesthetic devices present this issue in such a way that the reader is allowed to question it, questions its history and its authenticity. This is what allows for a political critique of the representation, not only our feelings as a society towards the elderly, but also about financial concerns and how individuals with money are cared for, and about, differently than others. This idea is carried further, and uses more stereotypes of aging, when Grampa realises he doesn't have enough money to help all those who need help. So what does he do? Apparently what all old people in the United States do, he goes on a seniors gambling junket.

Homer has figured out where his father is heading and hoping to stop him from losing the money, sets off in a desperate high speed pursuit. Driving rapidly down the highway, eyes focused intently on the road, Homer gasps and goes into a power slide in his vehicle as he tries desperately to make a last second left hand turn. He must have seen something, something important. The bus perhaps. As he screeches and squeals he completes the turn and pulls into…a Krusty Burger Fast Food Drive-thru. He hurriedly orders "a double cheese burger, onion rings, a large strawberry shake and for God's sake hurry!!" He makes it to the casino and screaming "noooooooooo", he watches his father win big at roulette. Trying to convince his father to quit while he's ahead, Homer is momentarily silenced by his father's impassioned speech.

> **Grampa**: I think Rudyard Kipling said it best: If you can make one heap of all your winnings and risk it on one turn of pitch-and-toss, and lose, and start again at your beginnings, [*by this point, soft emotional music is playing and the entire casino appears to have stopped to listen*] and never breathe a word about your loss, yours is the earth and everything that's it, and, which is more, you'll be a man, my son.
>
> **Homer**: You'll be a bonehead!
>
> **Grampa**: Put it all on 41. [*nudges Homer*] I've got a feeling about that number.
>
> **Roulette man**: The wheel only goes to 36 sir.
>
> **Grampa**: Okay, put it all on 36.
> [*nudges Homer*] I've got a feeling about that number.
> [*Homer stops his father from betting on 36. The ball ultimately ends up falling into the 00 slot, saving Grampa all his money*]

This scene references a portion of the inspirational Rudyard Kipling poem "If" and Abe is using it in this instance as well for inspirational purposes. An irony at work here is that Homer has saved his father's money by ignoring this inspirational plea, and as Abe goes on to mention, "for the first time in my life I'm glad I had children". And despite Homer's happiness at reconnecting with his father, he will simply take him back to the home and continue to ignore him in each subsequent episode.

As the program draws to a close, Homer sits outside, eating on a bench while his father sits all downtrodden, suitcase overflowing with money between his legs. In between bites, Homer asks "So uh…have you figured out who gets the money?" Watching his fellow Retirement Castle residents filing back onto their bus with their blue hair, shuffle steps, and walkers, Grampa pauses to stare at his wrinkled hands, and we see them close up, from his perspective. He stretches and clenches them before folding them and turning to his son. "Yes Homer, I have".

We see a shot of the aged home, falling apart and weather beaten. The roof is a patchwork quilt of materials, the awning hangs in tatters and the yard is overgrown and unwieldy. A title appears across the screen that says "SIX MONTHS LATER" as the home slowly begins to morph into a bright, fantastic, and restored version of what it once was. Residents frolic in the front yard, light cascades off of the shiny windows and perhaps most importantly, a new "Springfield Retirement Castle" sign hangs proudly, sans the "hide from the inevitable" tag line.

We go inside and see happy residents all sitting in new recliners, walls are painted, they are adorned with colourful artworks, and a new big screen TV is playing. The pool table is fixed, the ceiling isn't leaking, and books are lining the bookshelves. The opposite of how things were six months ago. A shiny gold plaque on the door reads "The Beatrice Simmons Memorial Dining Hall" in honour of Grampa's late girlfriend. The doors swing open to reveal an ornate room filled with tables and beautiful settings. Grampa steps up and announces to the crowd "Come on in. Dignity's on me, friends!" Thanks to *The Simpsons* and its ultimately positive look at aging, dignity is available for all aging people.

The representations of the elderly in "Old Money" follow rigid stereotypes and expectations, to the point of helping to show just how ridiculous they are. This is often the result of the satirization of these beliefs. For example, the sign in front of the retirement home which says "Where the elderly can hide from the inevitable" is mocking the idea that the elderly, at least those in homes, have no purpose left and are simply waiting for death's embrace. As we all know, while there are elderly people with health issues, we also know someone who is still spry, alert, and contributing to society. By painting an entire group with one ludicrous brush of homogeneity, it shows in a humorous fashion how wrong this portrayal ultimately is. The irony of course is that Abe's new girlfriend does not manage to hide from the inevitable as she passes away shortly after their first meeting.

The Simpsons utilize ironic parody and satire in these situations as a tool to be critical of the values and representations shown and despite Jameson's claims to the contrary, to help historicize them. By recognizing the history of these representations, by questioning their past and their legitimacy, it allows for more than simple imitation, but offers a political critique opening the door for these representations to be undermined or subverted. Why have we looked at the elderly as frail, helpless, lonely, and as a burden? *The Simpsons* portrays them as such, some of the time at least, but utilizing parodic and ironic devices within its postmodern aesthetic allows the viewer to question these representations by allowing the reader to adopt a critical eye.

CONCLUSION

Questions of aging are at the forefront in many disciplines. Studies in elder care, aging and environment, health care, social policy, and demography are burgeoning across the academic landscape. As our nation ages, questions and concerns emerge that need attention, and attention is now being paid. One issue of importance is media representations of the elderly, important for a number of reasons. In an era when politically correct language has been widely adopted, and when many groups in our social structure have asked for increased respect and gotten it for the most part, the elderly are still regularly derided and stereotyped in a negative fashion. While it is no longer socially acceptable to make disparaging jokes based on gender, ethnicity, or handicap, there exists a feeling that the elderly and their lives are still available to mock, often utilizing false concerns.

As the voluminous research demonstrates, the media plays an integral role in helping to both transmit and construct the ideological values that our society attribute to the aged. We don't have a particularly positive attribution to our elders. The research indicates that "we live in an ageist society, one in which the predominant attitude towards older people is coloured by a negative mixture of, pity, fear, disgust, condescension, and neglect (Biggs, 1989; Scrutton, 1990; as cited in Featherstone & Hepworth, 1995). Considering the important role that the media has, it is unfortunate that the truth about the aging process, and aging persons, are not regularly presented in the many pervasive media forms (Weaver, 1994). This is obviously problematic to many people and for many reasons. The elderly themselves express concern that media representations of their cohort don't realistically portray the existence that they live, serving to marginalize and silence the wisdom they possess while also fabricating negative ideas about growing old.

Whether a representation is real or not is seemingly irrelevant according to Michel Foucault (Hall, 1997) because if something is repeated enough, and most believe it to be true, it is true, at least in the sense that it has that affect on the discourse of our social world. It would appear to be true based on the research conducted in media representations of aging. The elderly are underrepresented in relation to their actual percentage in real life, they are shown primarily as frail, dependent, a social strain, and as non-productive within the larger social scheme (Evers, 1998; Featherstone & Hepworth, 1995; Featherstone & Wernick, 1995; Hareven, 1995; McPherson, 1998). The negative myths and exaggerations around aging have served to create a negative discourse on growing old that serve to marginalize and discriminate against this group, served to us through the media we consume.

It is these media—television, print, film, and music for example—that effectively present youth as the social norm, as the ultimate ideal to be achieved. Obviously then, the aged are at the opposite of the ideal and thus become abnormal (Lock, 1993). If youth is seen as good, then aging must be bad. The sheer volume of products that are offered to subvert growing old, are at the very least looking like growing old, are testament to this idea.

While some recent research suggests that new, positive images of aging are beginning to appear in popular media, these are tied to the view that aging baby boomers are a lucrative consumer market with little debt and available expendable resources

(Sawchuk, 1995; Tulle-Winton, 1999). This does not serve to subvert the negative ideology that exist around aging, it only serves to offer products for consumption that can help make the horrible aging process better. Perhaps most importantly of all, it is not the voice of the elderly that is being heard, someone has taken to speaking for them, and not necessarily with their best interests in mind, interested only in maximizing profits. As Sawchuck (1995) points out, those individuals over the age of 50 have financial control of half of the discretionary income in North America. This hasn't gone unnoticed, resulting in the recommodification of an age group that was ignored and pushed out to the margins just a short time ago. Amidst all these messages, mixed or otherwise, the elderly themselves have different views of their lives and experiences.

While we often look for indicators of age, both consciously and subconsciously, when we meet someone else (Featherstone & Hepworth, 1995), the elderly themselves do not find age as a central defining characteristic of who they are (Bradley & Longino, 2001). In fact, many don't seem themselves as old at all. Even when they identify those around them as elderly, they still tend to think of themselves as chronologically younger than they are. Rather than simply succumbing to the barrage of negative images they encounter, the elderly often rely more on internal feelings of identity and age. That is not to say, however, that these mostly negative images don't affect others adversely. While perhaps not internalizing the negative assumptions about age, it does indicate to the aging the views that the larger society possess towards them (Healey & Ross, 2002). Perhaps most importantly of all in the research is the idea that most elderly would simply like a more realistic look at their lives and experiences. *The Simpsons* doesn't offer a realistic look at aging and often uses negative portrayals of the elderly, so how can it possibly be examined as a positive site of aging?

The Simpsons has a fascinating history, one that invariably stretches past its original appearance in 1987 to earlier animation forms and generic conventions. Created as a response to a milieu of situation comedies like *Leave it to Beaver* and *Ozzie and Harriet,* incorporating some irreverent satirical elements from shows like *All In the Family* or *Sanford & Son*, Matt Groening has created a generic hybrid by also paying homage to animated programs like *The Flintstones* and *The Jetsons*. Creating a resurgence in prime time animation, *The Simpsons* were able to rework the generic conventions of the sitcom and with its positioning as an animated program, it is able to question the status quo and make what appears to be childlike, very adult, and very serious.

The Simpsons is an interesting and an important text to examine with regard to images of aging. It fulfils the "requisite" aesthetic requirements for postmodern labelling, has become a cultural stalwart, is loved by the young and old (as well as being equally derided), and is able to get away with social critiques that no other programs seem capable of matching. It has been specifically referred to, by Beard (2004) and many others, as an oppositional text that successfully subverts stereotypes and social conventions. One of these is "through its ironic use of pre-existing mass media stereotypes precisely in order to destabilize them" (p. 273). This is achieved through the use of its postmodern aesthetics, and the subversive power that postmodernism affords them.

While the aesthetic postmodern theoretical writings of Frederic Jameson are arguably the most cited in the field, they fail to properly address the ironic underpinning in postmodern texts like *The Simpsons*. The hyper-reflexivity, self-awareness, inter-textuality, and parodic elements in postmodern texts, and specifically here in *The Simpsons* are the integral components that move beyond the modern aesthetics based in realism and generic convention. These textual aesthetics serve to do more than simply label or categorize, they create an arena in which cultural critique and oppositional subversion can reside. While Jameson focuses on parody as a pastiche that lacks true critical power as he sees it as ahistorical rehashing of prior texts that rehash rather than confront. It is an aesthetic based in our culture of commodity, existing to move products and carry no larger imperative. Thus Jameson sees parody as benign of political power, unable to critique as appearance is all that matters. Of course, Linda Hutcheon makes the move past this by demonstrating how irony is employed in these texts in order to historicize, contextualize, and create stereotypical opposition.

Working with a different perspective on the "postmodern"—Hutcheon's focus is on production while Jameson's is on consumption—Hutcheon believes that due to its inherent mandate, postmodernism has to operate as a contradiction to modernism and that alone is where political power is born through the self-reflexive history of this contradiction. As Hutcheon shows, the function of postmodernism in general was to serve as a check against the claims of absolute knowledge found in modern metanarratives, and these postmodern texts can then point out how what we think is natural, is in fact a culturally constructed entity with no basis in "reality". By its very nature, postmodernism is a critique, and a political act. This is one way that postmodernism works to offer subversive readings. One way to highlight this potential is through the use of parodic irony.

Irony is the ingredient that moves Jameson's pastiche past the idea of blank parody and creates a text that can be decoded as oppositional and whose role is to question the conventional. Irony is seen as "the power to entertain widely divergent possible interpretations—to provoke the reader into seeing that there is a radical uncertainty surrounding the processes by which meaning get determined in texts and interpreted by readers" (Dane, J. A., 1991, p. 150). Using ironic parody underlines the ideology inherent in all representations, including the representations of the elderly, and inserts room for the denaturalization of the politics of these representations. By demonstrating the mediated nature of our images, we then question the "reality" and meanings that are not so natural after all. It is parody where we see a strong use of irony on *The Simpsons*.

Parody borrows from past texts and through this historicization shows the evolution in our representations and their ideological implications. Answering critics who suggest that parody is simply a pastiche of former images with no inherent political power, Hutcheon (1985, 1989) shows that's by highlighting the passage of time and subsequent historical representations, the political burden is met. While satire is utilized in *The Simpsons,* and effectively so, it is parody that recognizes, pays respect to, and ultimately serves to authorize the original text. As Chatman (2001) notes, it is seemingly a respect for the original text that results in its parodization. It simultaneously ridicules as it pays respect and homage. Irony functions within this schema to showcase the contradictions and asks for a critical evaluation. *The Simpsons* utilize ironic parody in such a way that representations are afforded a new contextual stationing, demanding the reader access their own base of knowledge in decoding the text. In his essay "Local Satire with a Global

Reach" Beard (2004) agrees with this thesis as he writes that the use of parodic representations on *The Simpsons* are purposeful and create a critique of American cultural ideals. As well, he suggests the use of satire also helps to undermine the "media-generated stereotypes through an interrogatory utilization of these same stereotypes with subversively ironic intent" (p. 288). These representations are thus problematized, removing the badge of "natural" and thus open for a critical re-evaluation.

So *The Simpsons* do employ negative representations of the elderly, the same representations railed against in the literature and research. While these familiar stereotypes exist with our larger social structure, and are repeated ad nauseam in our cultural texts, there exists a means by which these representations can become historicized, contextualized, probed, questioned, undermined, and potentially subverted. It is the opening of a critical discourse through the satiric and ironic parodizations of these representations on *The Simpsons* that we can look into the ideology that drives these portrayals on the mass media and in our culture. We can look at our representations of the elderly, question them, fight them, and as we understand better their basis in ideology, dispel them. It was Homer Simpson who said that "old people are useless", why does this feeling exist and how can we change it? Stay tuned for the next episode of *The Simpsons*, an answer may reside there.

BIBLIOGRAPHY

Aday, R. H., & Austin, B.S. (2000). Images of Aging in the Lyrics of American Country Music. *Educational Gerontology*. 26, 135-154.

Ahmad, R. (2002). The older or ageing consumers in the U.K.: Are they really that different? *International Journal of Marketing*. 44(3), 337-360.

Alberti, J. (2004). Introduction. In John Alberti (Ed.), *Leaving Springfield: The Simpsons and the possibility of oppositional culture*. Detroit: Wayne State University Press.

Al Gore vs. Bart Simpson. (2000). *Techniques: Connecting Education and Careers*. 75(1). 14.

Arac, J. (1986). *Postmodernism and politics*. Minneapolis, MN: University of Minnesota Press.

Auger, J. A., & Tedford-Litle, D. (2002). *From the inside looking out: Competing ideas about growing old*. Halifax: Fernwood.

Barney, C. (2003, February 15). Simpsons has proved it's the best. *Contra Costa Times*. Retrieved January 23, 2004, from http://www.contracostatimes.com/mld/cctimes/5189371.htm

Bauder, D. (2004). The top 20 American Nielsen Ratings. Retrieved March 25, 2004, from the Canoe.ca Web site: http://www.canoe.ca/TelevisionRatings/us.html

Beard, D. S. (2004). Local Satire with a Global Reach: Ethnic Stereotyping and Cross-Cultural Conflicts in The Simpsons. In John Alberti (Ed.), *Leaving Springfield: The Simpsons and the possibility of oppositional culture*. Detroit: Wayne State University Press.

Booth, W. (1974). *A rhetoric of irony*. Chicago: University of Chicago Press.

Bultena, G. L. & Powers, E. A. (1978). Denial of aging: Age identification and reference group orientation. *Journal of Gerontology*. 33, 748-754.

Bradley, D.E., & Longino, C.F. (2001). How older people think about images of aging in Advertising and the media. *Generations*. 25(3), 17-21.

Chaney, D. (1995). Creating memories: Some images of aging in mass tourism. In M. Featherstone & A. Wernick (eds.), *Images of Aging: Cultural Representations Of Later Life*. (pp. 209-224). New York, NY: Routledge.

Chatman, S. (2001). Parody and Style. *Poetics Today.* 22(1), 25-39.

Cohen, H. L. (2002). Developing media literacy skills to challenge television's portrayal of older women. *Educational Gerontology.* 28, 599-620.

Coupland, N., Coupland, J., & Giles, H. (1991). *Language, society and the elderly: discourse, identity, and ageing.* Cambridge, MASS: Blackwell.

Chrittenden, J. (1995, January 22). And Maggie Makes Three (S. O. Scott III, Director). In J. L. Brooks, M. Groening, & S. Simon (Executive Producers), *The Simpsons.* New York: Twentieth Century Fox Film Corporation.

D'Acci, J. (2004). Television, representation and gender. In R. C. Allen & A. Hill (Eds.), *The Television Studies Reader.* (pp. 367-388). New York, NY: Routledge.

Dail, P. (1988). Prime time television portrayals of older adults in the context of family life. *Gerontologist.* 28(5), 700-706.

Dane, J. A. (1991). *The critical mythology of irony.* Athens, GA: University of Georgia Press.

Davis, R. H., & Davis, J. A. (1985). *TV's image of the elderly: A practical guide for change.* Toronto: Lexington.

Dettmar, K. J. H. (2004). Learning irony with the Simpsons. In John Alberti (Ed.), *Leaving Springfield: The Simpsons and the possibility of oppositional culture.* Detroit: Wayne State University Press.

Dossa, P. A. (1999). (Re)imagining Aging Lives: Ethnographic Narratives of Muslim Women in Diaspora. *Journal of Cross-Cultural Gerontology.* 14, 245-272.

Duvall, J. (1999). Troping History: Modernist Residue in Fredric Jameson's Pastiche and Linda Hutcheon's Parody. *Style.* 33(3), 372-390.

Evers, H. (1998). *Aging and Mass Media. Wake up and Smell the Demographics: Silver Wave Swells.* [On-line]. Available at www.npoe.nl/doc/ageing.doc [2002, Nov 23].

Featherstone, M. & Hepworth, M. (1995). Images of Positive Aging: A Case Study of Retirement Choice Magazine. In M. Featherstone & A. Wernick (eds.), *Images of Aging: Cultural Representations Of Later Life.* (pp. 29-47). New York, NY: Routledge.

Featherstone, M. & Wernick, A. (1995). Introduction: Imaging the Aging Body. In M. Featherstone & A. Wernick (eds.), *Images of Aging: Cultural Representations Of Later Life*. (pp. 1-15). New York, NY: Routledge.

Feldman, S. (1999). Please don't call me 'dear': Older women's narratives of health care. *Nursing Inquiry*. 6, 269-276.

Fox's 'Simpsons' Closes In on NBC's 'Cosby' Ratings. (1990, October 15). *Wall Street Journal*, p. B10.

Gerbner, G., Gross, L., Signorielli, N., & Morgan, M. (1980). Aging with Television: Images of Television Drama and Conceptions of Social Reality. *Journal of Communication*. 30, 37-47.

Goldman, K. (1990a, May 30). CBS and Fox adopt risky strategies in fight to capture prime time crown. *Wall Street Journal*, p. B3.

Goldman, K. (1990b, September 10). TV networks bet quirky new programs, schedule changes will win back viewers. *Wall Street Journal*, p. B1.

Hall, S. (1980). Encoding/Decoding. In S. Hall, D. Hobson, A. Lowe, and P. Willis (eds.), *Culture, Media, Language: Working Papers in Cultural Studies*. London: Hutchinson Publishing.

Hall, S. (1997). *Representation: Cultural representations and signifying practices*. London: Sage Publications.

Hareven, T. K. (1995). Changing Images of Aging and the Social Construction of the Life Course. In M. Featherstone & A. Wernick (eds.), *Images of Aging: Cultural Representations Of Later Life*. (pp. 119-134). New York, NY: Routledge.

Harwood, J. (2000). Sharp!: Lurking Incoherence in a Television Portrayal of an Older Adult. *Journal of Language & Social Psychology*. 19(1), 110-141.

Healey, T. & Ross, K. (2002). Growing Old Invisibly: Older Viewers Talk Television. *Media, Culture & Society*. 24, 105-120.

Hilton-Morrow, W. & McMahan, D. T. (2003). The Flintstones to Futurama: Networks and prime time animation. In C. A. Stabile & M. Harrison (Eds.), *Prime Time Animation: Television animation and American Culture*. New York: Routledge.

Hocking, T. & Rose, M. (2003). *Alt.tv.simpsons - List of Inquiries and Substantive Answers: Series Background*. [Online]. Available http://www.snpp.com/guides/lisa.html [2004, Jan 29]

Hoesterey, I. (1999). From Genre Mineur to Critical Aesthetic: Pastiche. *European Journal of English Studies*. 3(1). 78-86.

Hofstetter, C.R., & Schultze, W.A. (1993). The elderly's perception of TV ageist stereotyping: TV or contextual aging? *Communication Reports*. 6(2), 92-100.

Holstein, J. A. & Gubrium. J. F. (2000). *The self we live by: Narrative identity in a postmodern world*. New York: Oxford University Press.

Hutcheon, L. (1989). *The politics of postmodernism*. New York: Routledge.

Jameson, F. (1984a). The Politics of Theory: Ideological Positions in the Postmodern Debate. *New German Critique*. 33. 53-65.

Jameson, F. (1984b). Postmodernism or, the cultural logic of late capitalism. *New Left Review*. 146. 53-91.

Jameson, F. (1991). *Postmodernism or, the cultural logic of late capitalism*. Durham: Duke University Press.

Jean, A & Mike Reiss. (1992, January 30). Stark Raving Dad (R. Moore, Director). In J. L. Brooks, M. Groening, & S. Simon (Executive Producers), *The Simpsons*. New York: Twentieth Century Fox Film Corporation.

Keeler, K. (1995, March 5). A Star Is Burns (S. Dietter, Director). In J. L. Brooks, M. Groening, & S. Simon (Executive Producers), *The Simpsons*. New York: Twentieth Century Fox Film Corporation.

Kellner, D. (1997). Fredric Jameson. In M. Groden & M. Kreiswirth (Eds.), *The John Hopkins Guide to Literary Theory & Criticism*. Baltimore, MD: John Hopkins University Press.

Kogen, J. & W. Wolodarsky. (1990, December 6th). Bart the Daredevil. (W. M. Archer, Director). In J. L. Brooks, M. Groening, & S. Simon (Executive Producers), *The Simpsons*. New York: Twentieth Century Fox Film Corporation.

Kogen, J. & W. Wolodarsky. (1991, March 28th). Old Money. (D. Silverman, Director). In J. L. Brooks, M. Groening, & S. Simon (Executive Producers), *The Simpsons*. New York: Twentieth Century Fox Film Corporation.

Lock, Margaret, M. (1993). Epilogue: The Politics of Aging—Flashes of Immortality. *Encounters With Aging: Mythologies of Menopause in Japan and North America*. (pp. 370-387). US: University of California Press.

Lyotard, J. (1984). *The postmodern condition: A report on knowledge.* Minneapolis, MN: University of Minnesota Press.

Mares, M-L. & Cantor, J. (1992). Elderly Viewer's Responses to Televised Portrayals of Old Age. *Communication Research.* 19(4), 459-479.

Markson, E. W. & Taylor, C. A. (2000). The Mirror Has Two Faces. *Ageing and Society.* 20, 137-160.

Martin-Matthews, A. (1999). Canada and the Changing Profile of Health and Social Services: Implications for Employment and Caregiving. In V. M. Lechner & M. B. Neal (Eds.), *Work and Caring for the Elderly: International Perspectives* (pp.11-28). Philadelphia, PA: Brunner/Mazel.

Mason, M. S. (1998). Simpsons creator on poking fun. *Christian Science Monitor.* 90(99), B7.

McPherson, B. D. (1998). *Aging as a Social Process (Third Edition).* Toronto: Harcourt Brace.

Mead, G. H. (1934). *Mind, Self, and Society.* Chicago: University of Chicago Press.
Robinson, J. D. & Skill, T. (1995). The Invisible Generation: Portrayals of the Elderly on Prime time Television. *Communication Reports.* 8(2), 111-120.

Milner, A. & Browitt, J. (2002). *Contemporary cultural theory, an introduction.* (3rd ed.). New York: Routledge.

Mittell, J. (2001). Cartoon Realism: Genre Mixing and the Cultural Life of the Simpsons. *The Velvet Light Trap.* 47, 15-28.

Mittell, J. (2003). The Great Saturday Morning Exile. In C. A. Stabile & M. Harrison (Eds.), *Prime Time Animation: Television animation and American Culture.* New York: Routledge.

Mullen, M. (2004). The Simpsons and Hanna-Barbera's Animation Legacy. In John Alberti (Ed.), *Leaving Springfield: The Simpsons and the possibility of oppositional culture.* Detroit: Wayne State University Press.

Nielsen Media Research. (2004). [Online]. Available: http://www.nielsenmedia.com/ [2004, Jan 18].

Newcomb, H. (2000). Television: The critical view. In Horace Newcomb (Ed.). New York: University of Oxford Press.

Oakley, B. & . Josh Weinstein. (1994, Feb. 17). Lisa vs., Malibu Stacy. (J. Lynch, Director). In J. L. Brooks, M. Groening, & S. Simon (Executive Producers), *The Simpsons*. New York: Twentieth Century Fox Film Corporation.

Oakley, B. & . Josh Weinstein. (1994, May 12). Lady Bouvier's Lover (W. Archer, Director). In J. L. Brooks, M. Groening, & S. Simon (Executive Producers), *The Simpsons*. New York: Twentieth Century Fox Film Corporation.

Ott, B. L. (2003). "I'm Bart Simpson, who the hell are you?" A study in Postmodern Identity (re)Construction. *The Journal of Popular Culture*. 37(1). 56-81.

Owens, T. O. & Goodney, S. (2000). Self, identity, and the moral emotions across the life course. In T. J. Owens (Ed.), *Self and identity through the life course in cross-cultural perspective*. Stamford, CONN: JAI Press Inc.

Palys, T. (1997). *Research Decisions: Qualitative and Quantitative Perspectives*. London, UK: Harcourt Brace.

Robinson, J. D. & Skill, T. (1995). The Invisible Generation: Portrayals of the Elderly on Prime time Television. *Communication Reports*. 8(2), 111-120.

Rose, L. (2004). *The Flintstones – TV Series – TV Tome*. [Online]. Available: http://www.tvtome.com/tvtome/servlet/ShowMainServlet/showid-3642/ [2004, Jan 26].

Rose, M. (2003). The Simpsons Archive: Episode Guide. Behind the Laughter. [On-Line]. Available: http://www.snpp.com/episodes/BABF19 [2004, Feb. 3].

Rosel, N. (2001). Inconspicuous Consumption: How a Small Sample of Rural Elders See Images in the Media. Generations. 25(3), 47-51.

Roy, A. & Harwood, J. (1997). Underrepresented, positively portrayed: Older adults in television commercials. *Journal of Applied Communication Research*. 25, 39-56.

Rushkoff, D. (2004). Bart Simpson: Prince of Irreverence. In John Alberti (Ed.), *Leaving Springfield: The Simpsons and the possibility of oppositional culture*. Detroit: Wayne State University Press.

Ryan, A. J. (1992). Postmodern Parody: A Political Strategy in Contemporary Canadian Native Art. *Art Journal*. 51(3), 59-65.

Savage Jr., W. J. (2004). "So Television's Responsible!". In John Alberti (Ed.), *Leaving Springfield: The Simpsons and the possibility of oppositional culture*. Detroit: Wayne State University Press.

Sawchuk, K. A. (1995). From Gloom to Boom: Age, Identity and Target Marketing. In M. Featherstone & A. Wernick (Eds.), *Images of Aging: Cultural Representations Of Later Life*. New York: Routledge.

Schmidt, S. (2003, November 19). D'oh! Homer makes the grade. *The Calgary Herald*, p. A13.

Sherman, E. (1991). *Reminiscence and the self in old age*. New York, NY: Springer Publishing Company.

Signorielli, N. (2001). Aging on Television: The Picture in the Nineties. *Generations*. 25(3), 34-38.

Simpsons broke new ground for cartoons. (2002, July 13). *Halifax Daily News*, p. 26.

Statistics Canada, 2001 Census: Age and Sex Profile. (2001). [On-line] Available: http://www12.statcan.ca/english/census01/products/analytic/companion/age/canada.cf m [2002, Nov 21].

Statistics Canada, 2001 Census: Population by age group. (2001). [On-Line] Available: http://www.statcan.ca/english/Pgdb/demo31a.htm. [2002, Nov 22].

Statistics Canada, Population projections. (2002). [On-Line] Available: http://www.statcan.ca/english/Pgdb/demo23b.htm. [2002, Nov 21].

Statistics Canada, TV in the Life of the Canadian Family. (2002). [On-line] Available: http://www.statcan.ca/english/kits/winner/2001/tv/inthelife.htm [2002, Dec 3].

Stern, D. M. (1992, September 24). Kamp Krusty (M. Kirkland, Director). In J. L. Brooks, M. Groening, & S. Simon (Executive Producers), *The Simpsons*. New York: Twentieth Century Fox Film Corporation.

Storey, J. (1998). *An introduction to cultural theory and popular culture*. Athens, GA: University of Georgia Press.

Swartzwelder, J. (1991, October 10). Bart the Murderer (R. Moore, Director). In J. L. Brooks, M. Groening, & S. Simon (Executive Producers), *The Simpsons*. New York: Twentieth Century Fox Film Corporation.

Swartzwelder, J. (1994, January 6). Homer the Vigilante (J. Reardon, Director). In J. L. Brooks, M. Groening, & S. Simon (Executive Producers), *The Simpsons*. New York: Twentieth Century Fox Film Corporation.

Thacker, J. (1999, April 25). The Old Man and the C student (M. Kirkland, Director). In J. L. Brooks, M. Groening, & S. Simon (Executive Producers), *The Simpsons*. New York: Twentieth Century Fox Film Corporation.

The Golden Girls. (2003). *Titles and airdates guide*. [On-Line]. Available: http://epguides.com/GoldenGirls/ [2004, Apr. 19].

Todd, A. M. (2002). Prime time Subversion: The Environmental Rhetoric of The Simpsons. In M. Meister & P. M. Japp (Eds.), *Enviropop: Studies in Environmental Rhetoric and Popular Culture*. Westport, Conn: Praeger.

Tulle-Winton, E. (1999). Growing Old and Resistance: Towards a New Cultural Economy of Old Age? *Ageing and Society*. 19, 281-299.

US Census Bureau. The Elderly Population. (1994). [On-line] Available: http://www.census.gov/population/www/pop-profile/elderpop.html [2002, Nov 29].

Waiting for God. (2003). *British TV Comedy*. [On-Line]. Available: http://www.phill.co.uk/comedy/waitgod/ [2004, Apr. 19].

Weaver, J. W. (1999). Gerontology Education: A New Paradigm for the 21st Century. Educational Gerontology. 25(6), 479-491.